Pathways to Belonging

Pathways to Belonging

EDITED BY
Dustin D. Benac,
Erin Weber-Johnson,
AND Glen Bell

WITH A FOREWORD BY
Willie James Jennings

CASCADE Books · Eugene, Oregon

PATHWAYS TO BELONGING

Copyright © 2025 Wipf and Stock Publishers. All rights reserved. Except for brief quotations in critical publications or reviews, no part of this book may be reproduced in any manner without prior written permission from the publisher. Write: Permissions, Wipf and Stock Publishers, 199 W. 8th Ave., Suite 3, Eugene, OR 97401.

Cascade Books
An Imprint of Wipf and Stock Publishers
199 W. 8th Ave., Suite 3
Eugene, OR 97401

www.wipfandstock.com

PAPERBACK ISBN: 979-8-3852-0332-1
HARDCOVER ISBN: 979-8-3852-0333-8
EBOOK ISBN: 979-8-3852-0334-5

Cataloguing-in-Publication data:

Names: Benac, Dustin D., editor. | Weber-Johnson, Erin, editor. | Bell, Glen, editor. | Jennings, Willie James, 1961–, foreword.

Title: Pathways to belonging / edited by Dustin D. Benac, Erin Weber-Johnson, and Glen Bell ; foreword by Willie James Jennings.

Description: Eugene, OR : Cascade Books, 2025 | Includes bibliographical references.

Identifiers: ISBN 979-8-3852-0332-1 (paperback) | ISBN 979-8-3852-0333-8 (hardcover) | ISBN 979-8-3852-0334-5 (ebook)

Subjects: LCSH: Identity (Psychology)—Religious aspects—Christianity. | Experience (Religion). | Belonging (Social psychology). | Faith—Social aspects.

Classification: BL50 .P43 2025 (paperback) | BL50 .P43 (ebook)

VERSION NUMBER 04/01/25

Cover art by Leslie Barlow.
For more information, see https://www.lesliebarlowartist.com.

We dedicate this book to all who chase and foster belonging from the past, present, and future. May your pathway bring renewed connection and life.

Contents

Foreword: The Election of Belonging | xi
—Willie James Jennings

Acknowledgments | xv

Introduction: An Invitation: Pathways of Christian Belonging | xvii
—Dustin D. Benac, Erin Weber-Johnson, Glen Bell

Part 1: Ancestors

1 My Grandmother's Face: An Opportunity to Redefine Belonging | 3
—Erin Weber-Johnson

2 Keepers of Generational Fire | 10
—Patrick B. Reyes

3 Belonging in the Middle of Nowhere | 15
—Eric D. Barreto

Part 2: Identity

4 Too Many Cooks: Love, Otherwise | 25
—Mihee Kim-Kort

5 Fostering Belonging Through Afrofuturist Speculative Design: Co-Powering Just Futures with BIPOC Youth | 32
—Michael Dando

6 Yearning for Home: More Than I Know, More Than I Am | 43
—Glen Bell

7   Lydia Amid the Jewish Diaspora: Apostolic Migration and Belonging—Then and Now | 51
    —Amos Yong

Part 3: Risk

8   In the Beginning Were Autistic People and They Belonged | 61
    —Armand Léon Van Ommen and Krysia Waldock

9   When "Yes" Means "No": A Lament for Shattered Belonging | 68
    —Hannah Coe

10 AI and Belonging | 76
    —Eve Poole

Part 4: Practice

11 It's Good to Be Seen | 85
    —De'Amon Harges

12 Longing to Belong By Name | 93
    —Andrew Pomerville

13 Becoming the Body: Belonging in Paul's Letters and Today | 98
    —Zen Hess

Part 5: Barriers and Rupture

14 Beyond Assimilation, Toward a Story of "You Belong Here" | 109
    —Chris Dela Cruz

15 Transformative Belonging in Higher Education | 116
    —Kevin J. Villegas

16 How the Church Becomes the Heart of the Community: Risking Subversive Belonging Together | 123
    —Janelle Lindsay Adams

Part 6: Creation

17 On Seeing and Being Seen: Holy Portraits, Presence,
    and Belonging | 133
    —Jennifer Awes Freeman

18 Voice and Verse: Breathing and Belonging Together | 146
    —Craig Lemming

19 Cultural Humility as a Pathway to Belonging | 153
    —B. Hunter Farrell

20 A Music-Making Counter-Community | 161
    —Walter Brueggemann

Conclusion: Belonging in the Valley of Dry Bones | 168
    —Dustin D. Benac, Erin Weber-Johnson, Glen Bell

With our deepest gratitude to this volume's contributors:

Janelle Lindsay Adams
Eric D. Barreto
Glen Bell
Dustin D. Benac
Walter Brueggemann
Hannah Coe
Chris Dela Cruz
Michael Dando
B. Hunter Farrell
Jennifer Awes Freeman
De'Amon Harges
Zen Hess

Willie James Jennings
Mihee Kim-Kort
Craig Lemming
Andrew Pomerville
Eve Poole
Patrick B. Reyes
Armand Léon Van Ommen
Kevin J. Villegas
Krysia Waldock
Erin Weber-Johnson
Amos Yong

Foreword

The Election of Belonging

WILLIE JAMES JENNINGS

YOU HAVE TO DECIDE you want this. Some things in life are given to us, even pressed upon us—family, clan, tribe, nation, story, drama, quest, historical burden, responsibility. But some things must be chosen with a depth of commitment that reorders a life and reorganizes desire. Christian belonging is precisely that thing that must be chosen. It costs everything to choose to belong in this new way. But what does it mean to choose Christian belonging? This remains, sadly, a mystery to too many people who should understand it. This is a not a good mystery, like the triune life, the love of God, or the divine-human reality of Jesus of Nazareth. This is a sad mystery that shows our missed opportunities to follow the Spirit of the living God as the Spirit moves through the creation, calling and inviting us to communion. The mystery is why we resist participating in the desire of God, the same desire that formed creation, the same desire shown in the incarnation, the same desire that raised Jesus from the dead, and the same desire that baptized us into the flowing life of God.

To choose this belonging is to choose to become intoxicated with the desire of God, the desire to form in us an ever-expanding belonging. God desires to draw us into a life—let's call it a holy life—of connecting, enmeshing, burden-sharing, and building. God's desire for belonging invades other forms of belonging. This is a lesson that we have not grasped. Christianity botched this lesson almost from the beginning and quickly started turning every other form of belonging into its enemy. There were certainly forms of belonging that would not in practice tolerate a new form of belonging born of following Jesus into the life of the God of Israel. But too often we read the room poorly, confusing what God was doing with what God was prohibiting.

We meet in Jesus not a God who destroys the ties of belonging but loosens them. Even his most severe statements about hating father, mother, sister, brother, and even our own life are not statements that shatter the ties of belonging but untie them at the site of our bodies so that, with strings in hand, we may begin to tie them differently, beginning with tying them to Jesus. Yet something remarkable happens the moment we tie our life to Jesus. We come to realize that we are fundamentally glorious string. Our bodies and minds are string.

> I, the yarn, refuse the ball
> preferring the knot.
> I am moving breath, in and
> out of places, weaving people
> into my uncharted journey,
> being woven into their
> peregrinations sure of
> only one thing,
> I am the fold.

We come to realize that like Jesus, with Jesus, we are loose lines, and, as I suggest in this poem, poised to be woven with others, prepared to extend belonging. This is dangerous, risky living and being. As dangerous and risky as God becoming vulnerable string-flesh. We have always struggled with this living and being because by its very nature it is un-chartable, unpredictable, and wholly new, formed of the particulars of time, place, people, practice, and hope. We see glimpses of the logic of loose lines with some of Paul's famous statements to the Christians at Corinth, like, "I have become all things to all people, that I might by all means save some" (1 Cor 9:22b), or "For all things are yours" (3:21b), or "'All things are permitted,' but not all things are beneficial" (10:23a). Ties have been loosened and Paul is trying to understand how to work with those loosened ties.

We, too, are trying to learn to work with the loosened ties of belonging for the sake of new belonging. This is where the history of Christianity carries both the testimony of life giving new belonging and the record of belonging's destruction, mutilation, or weaponization. We have too often pitted Christian belonging against being part of family, clan, people, land, animal, ancestors, practices, rituals, and story. We have too often made Christian belonging into a prison that strips us of all ties and burdens us with a string that forms only a ball, ever turning only into itself. The bad record of Christian belonging modulated into horrific form with colonial Christianity and the arrival of racial belonging. With racial belonging, we entered a white waste land that we are yet to escape where belonging became a property, and life became a series of enclosures that run from the body to our families, from our peoples to nations, from our labor to our loving.

This history of racial belonging is still being written. Yet it exists alongside the testimony that is still ongoing of a God who desires and who even amid racial belonging, and all other forms of belonging is calling, inviting us to loosen our strings and tie them to God's holy child, Jesus. This calling is nothing less than divine election, of God choosing us in Jesus, choosing to become string-flesh in order to make many mothers, many siblings, and many lifelong friends, all becoming ever-weaving flesh through the Spirit. Election, however, requires election. It requires those who are willing to expand affection, care, concern, commitment beyond the givens of family, clan, people, nation, religion, land, and animal. It requires those who are willing to yield to the Spirit in restoring the majesty of a revolutionary intimacy. That intimacy forms in a project of living together with difference, accepting new ways of being in the world with new peoples. This is ultimately what church, what the gathering is supposed to be, the presentation of Jesus's body extending strings into the lives of all and allowing the lives of all to extend into the life of God.

This is why modern coupling is so problematic and the idea of the nuclear or immediate family so potentially idolatrous. Both have colonized belonging. Both would shorten the strings of belonging and turn our imaginations to a future of relational cul-de-sacs. Too much of our dreaming of love and care has been swallowed up in coupling, in a romanticism and sentimentalism that we have made salvific. Too much community life has been surrendered to the supremacy of the couple, who have moved their life and their love to the center of our existence, draining Christian belonging of its inheritance, its power, and its calling. The sovereign couple must be resisted if we, especially in the western world, would know our own string-flesh. This is the unfinished business of Christian belonging.

These essays show us the struggle of belonging at the sites of family, faith, religion, peoplehood, education, and identity, and in so doing mark the urgent task of forming belonging against the strong head winds of isolationist and segregationist practice. The task, therefore, is not simply to form belonging but to enter the new possibilities of a belonging that would remake the world. The world may be remade through forming new ties, founding new knots, that will not be untied by the machinations of capitalism, the military power of nation-states, or the political maneuvering of corporations. This is belonging that feeds the hungry, houses the homeless, heals the broken, and gives hope to the hopeless. This belonging does not end. It is always just the beginning of endless string, always unfolding, like a scroll being read in a temple that holds an eternal word being spoken in flesh.

Willie James Jennings

Sixth Day of Christmas
Hamden, Connecticut

Acknowledgments

Even as this is a collaborative work, we each wish to acknowledge particular people and communities who shaped our ability to imagine and pursue belonging.

From Erin:

With gratitude, to my grandparents, Robert & Arlene Weber and Emery & Mary Ann Broschat.

From Glen:

With gratitude, to my parents, Doug and Susie Bell.

From Dustin:

With gratitude to my children, Cade, Ellie, and Ames. May your lives be filled by the reality of belonging.

I also wish to express gratitude to Lilly Endowment, Inc., for supporting an initial convening about belonging through the "Future Church Project" grant to Baylor University's George W. Truett Theological Seminary.

Finally, we offer our deepest gratitude to the contributors to this volume. Thank you for offering your words and witness through these meditations, inviting others to take the risk belonging requires.

Introduction

An Invitation

Pathways of Christian Belonging

Dustin D. Benac, Erin Weber-Johnson, and Glen Bell

Belonging is the air we breathe. It isn't *like* the air; it is the very oxygen that fills our lungs. We do not exist apart from one another. We cannot breathe without the people, places, and values that form our lives. When we inhale, our bodies acknowledge our dependence on others. Belonging, like the air we breathe, permeates the fullness of our existence. We exist in a symbiotic and enduring state of mutuality, giving and receiving our breath from others, finding our place amid our present creaturely existence. When we exhale, we offer our life, our sense of self, our hopes and intentions out into the world. We belong to each other, and we belong to God; this is the fundamental reality that grounds and forms our lives, making all other life possible.

Belonging is the air we breathe.

This pattern of life-giving and life-receiving existence can order our individual and collective bodies in holy and hopeful ways. A healthy sense of belonging provides structure where individuals and communities are able to imagine what's possible, take chances, and give life to the next generation. We cannot imagine our life in relation to others without the ancestors that came before us and the great communion that surrounds us. As we acknowledge the power of belonging in our past and present, we offer our lives, our ideas, and our gifts to the world. Through these commitments we learn to give and receive belonging as we lean into the future with great hope.

Like air, belonging is also a matter of life and death. We need air to survive, and we need a sense of belonging to live. Researchers have identified belonging as a key indicator of flourishing, wellbeing, educational success, and mental health.[1] Belonging is essential for the life of faith, and the passing down of faith from one generation to the next. A sense of belonging is a fundamental feature of individual and collective existence, but the very thing we know we need for life does not always fill our lives and communities. We do not always receive the gift of the air we breathe. Instead, we move through the world breathless or gasping for air, while others silently endure the suffocating consequences that come from a lack of belonging.

We carry a fractured and fragmented sense of belonging that leaves us wounded and weary, looking for a people to call our people and a place to call home, and unable to extend the belonging that is necessary for life to others. When our sense of belonging is uncertain, it functions like a parasite within the core of our being. It slowly eats away at what we need to live, thrive, and grow, and then renders us increasingly unable to extend ourselves to offer belonging to others. As our inner life grows thin, we grow less able and willing to extend to others the trust, kindness, and attentiveness that emerges from and contributes to belonging. We pray less, become cynical, and begin to question (and possibly even despise) those that are closest to us. We grow weary of institutional life and begin to wonder if it is better, or simply easier, to go alone. The absence of belonging will not only slowly kill our bodies and our souls, it will turn each of us into a death-dealing presence that can suck the life and soul out of individuals and communities. We become the walking dead, people and communities who live only by taking life and belonging from others.

Belonging is a matter of life and death.

Finally, belonging is also the question of this generation. The cascading crises of the pandemic, economic challenges, January 6, and the toxic soup of racism, sexism, and ableism has led to a liminal moment in our common life. Today, the United States faces another polarizing election. Through it all, we are caring for families and loved ones, discerning the nature of community, and trying to imagine a common life amid dizzying technological changes. We inhabit a particular moment, and yet we also move through

---

1. For a helpful introduction to interdisciplinary research, see Cohen, *Belonging*.

this time in our individual and collective life without fully knowing what time we are in, much less where and how to belong.[2]

Belonging is the question of a generation. This question requires considering, among others: How do our shared practices, values, and beliefs shape our common existence? How do we define and articulate what belonging is . . . and isn't? How do we determine its shape and boundaries? How do we create the deep trust that fosters its growth? And how do we create communities of holy listening and reflection when the congregations, denominations, schools, and political parties on which we have long relied, are now being transformed by destructive processes that reconfigure how we gather?

Every generation must determine the form of belonging that makes a common life possible. This negotiation occurs in the public and private spaces of our lives. The generational question of belonging is negotiated and shared amid the ordinary, everyday, and often unseen moments of life: In these small spaces of encounter the fabric of belonging is being crafted and carried from one life to another.

The meditations in this volume are attuned to the life-giving reality of belonging. Each author witnesses to the essentials of individual and collective life. We long to belong, and the testimonies here draw wisdom from our ancestors, plumb the riches of this present moment, and point the way to the future. Each chapter speaks a vital word in this matter of life and death. And even though a deeper belonging often seems just over the horizon, there are pathways here to a better day.

Belonging: An Invitation to a Reality

As there is a vast and complex body of research about belonging, some definitions are in order. By "belonging" we refer to a reality of interconnectedness that allows us to find a place that orients our desires for others, both those near to us and those who follow us, within a tradition of good practice.

This definition of belonging is thicker and stronger than other related accounts. We think belonging is more than a "sense" or a "feeling,"[3]

---

2. Andy Root's description of *dispositif,* a constellation of scattered practices, discourses, artifacts, and beliefs, provides a resonant description of the marked and liminal time we inhabit (Root, *Church After Innovation,* 139–41).

3. For example, a Springtide report on belonging defines belongingness as "the State

although both of those are important aspects of belonging. Instead, it is an anchoring and orienting reality, a state of existence that contains within it a set of possibilities—and relationships—that demand something of us and make ways of belief and belonging possible. The way of life that emerges from belonging cultivates a hopeful imagination, and allows us to tell the truth about the promise and peril of Christian belonging.

Five features of this definition detail the central properties of how we understand belonging. First, belonging is a reality of interconnectedness. As Geoffrey Cohen notes, belonging emerges when "we're part of a larger group that values, respects, and cares for us—and to which we feel we have something to contribute."[4] We long to be connected with others, and relational connectedness is needed to survive. Amid mounting loneliness and polarization,[5] the interconnectedness that is required for life, faith, and imagination is essential for our individual and collective life. Belonging emerges when we see the connections that make life possible and the ways these connections cross time and places.

Second, belonging is a concrete reality. We navigate belonging in and through the dirt of our material existence. Because it is a local and material reality, belonging allows us to find our place alongside others. Belonging is, as bell hooks notes, "a culture of place,"[6] one in which individuals-in-communities are grounded in a matrix of relationships. The local and material quality of belonging, what we have described as a place, locates belonging in relation to concrete spaces we inhabit, as well as to the realities and places of displacement. There is a certain "gravity" to belonging, a material weight that roots us in place and invites us to consider how displacement through forced immigration, exile, and gentrification complicates and reconfigures belonging.

Third, belonging is an affective reality. It is, as Teri Ott notes, a "whiff of home."[7] We often feel belonging before we can always articulate it. Even when the reality does not evoke memories of belovedness and care,

---

of feeling connectedness that arises when seen, known, and accepted by others" (7). Eastwood's *Belonging* notes: "To feel a sense of belonging is to feel accepted, to feel seen and to feel included by a group of people, believing that we fit in, trusting we will be protected by them" (22).

4. Cohen, *Belonging*, 5. While there is much to commend about Cohen's work, he describes belonging as a "feeling." We've purposefully reached beyond him in this regard.

5. Murthy, *Together*.

6. hooks, *belonging*.

7. Ott, "Whiff of Home."

we know when it is missing, and we know the real thing from poorer imitations. For this reason, it is a reality that frames and orients our desires, both for those we call our own and those we may experience as enemies. It is, as Willie James Jennings notes, the "desire of belonging,"[8] that makes a common life possible.

Fourth, belonging is a reality of relatedness to those near to us and to those who follow us. To belong is to recognize that we exist—and find our existence—only in relation to others and for those who follow us. While the ability to find a new space to belong for others is not unique to the Christian tradition, it is a central aspect of this religious tradition. One of the central claims of the gospel message is that we do not belong to ourselves. "You are not your own," writes the author of 1 Corinthians. The social reality that emerges in and through Christ entails "being-for-each-other,"[9] entering an ecology of belonging that crosses time and space. Belonging, in this sense, is generational. Even as we encounter belonging in amid the people and places that are near to us, in this particular spot of time, we receive and pass along belonging as one member in a long line of relatedness. Belonging is the work of being and becoming an ancestor.[10]

The interrelatedness that emerges through Christ—and the place-based practices that ground a faith community—introduces a future-oriented reciprocity. We discover belonging in relation to others, and we convey belonging by living for our future relations, even those we will not know.

Finally, belonging is a reality that exists because of the passing of good practice from generation to generation and culture to culture. Following from the first four aspects of this definition, this fifth feature places belonging within a broader social and historical frame. We know what belonging looks like and feels like because we have seen, felt, and experienced it. We know what it takes to belong to our people and our place because others have shown us. And the fabric of belonging has worked its way into us because of the things we do together—the practices that mark and direct our lives—and those practices that we don't do. For example, we know to sing

---

8. Jennings, *Christian Imagination*, 273. Jennings has written and spoken extensively about the formation of Christian belonging. For two examples, see "Belonging: A Conversation Between Willie Jennings and Eric Barreto," in Jennings, *After Whiteness*.

9. Bonhoeffer, *Sanctorum Communio*, 182. Bonhoeffer continues in the section that follows by introducing belonging as a theme: "Since I as a Christian cannot live without the church, since I owe my life to the church and now belong to it, so my merits are also no longer my own, but belong to the church" (183).

10. Reyes, *Purpose Gap*.

this way and not that way when we are among our people. We know how to greet others when we see them. And we know how to honor the boundaries of right action, belief, and connection that mark the reality of belonging. This is what we mean by a tradition of good practice.

Belonging is also carried by an infused understanding of what counts as good practice and a good life. Belonging is a morally laden reality that has embedded within it explicit and implicit understandings of what it means to belong. In this sense, belonging is a reality that exists because it is passed from one generation to the next through a shared understanding of good practice.

If belonging is a reality that exists because of the passing of good practice from generation to generation and culture to culture, it means that this process of generational and cultural transmission creates and requires different contexts of belonging. While belonging often requires some form of differentiation, and possibly even division, we are each drawing upon the life-giving reality of belonging to pass on a particular sense of good practice from one generation to the next.

At this point, it is important to note that even though belonging exists within generational transmission of good practice, belonging has virtuous and vicious expressions. If belonging is the air we breathe, if it is a question of life and death for this and every generation, then everyone needs this life-giving reality to survive. All people. All communities. In every time and place.[11]

Pathways to Christian Belonging

If the reality of belonging emerges from particular people, places, and communities, we cannot draw life apart from a broader community of practice and without the stories that make a common life possible. Hence, we purposefully invite a series of meditations about the making and unmaking of Christian belonging that draw wisdom from the particularity of lived experience. As first introduced in our collaborative volume, *Crisis and Care: Meditations on Faith and Philanthropy*, we purposefully describe the contributions as "meditations." Each chapter offers a contextually rooted and story-driven word on points that emerges from the author's particular

---

11. Our use of "circles" here to describe belonging draw on Murthy's description of the need for "circles of connection" (*Together*, 211–42).

work, ministry, or lived experience.[12] This approach to individual and collective storytelling presents a mosaic of belonging across time, contexts, and religious traditions as individuals and communities attempt to make meaning of a life lived in relation to God. Amid our contemporary crisis and longing for belonging, the meditations offered here provide a pathway to resource and renew belonging. We cannot discuss belonging in a rich, complex, and complete way without sharing meditations from authors who rub up against each other.

The combination of these meditations both provide a contextually-centered collection of stories for future research on belonging, as well as pathways to imagination for alternative practices and structures of belonging. The meditations offered here aim to examine and enrich the fabric of Christian belonging, as well as contribute to a broader conversation beyond this single religious tradition about the practice and study of belonging. These meditations come from leading researchers and visionary practitioners that carry a hopeful imagination about the possibility of Christian belonging, even amid the various perils and challenges that threaten this life-giving reality. In turn, the combination of these meditations here intend to catalyze and enliven the form(s) of social architecture that belonging requires. We've compiled them here to call for the breath that gives life to our individual and collective bodies, bearing witness by bodying forth the forms of belonging that allow us to kindle and carry a hopeful imagination.

The combination here has three consequences amid the contemporary crisis of belonging. First, they illustrate how individuals and communities are drawing the breath of life that belonging offers, even amid disorienting realities and fractured states of social existence. The narratives compiled here illustrate how the call to life—and the call to belong—can supersede competing narratives that seek to diminish and fragment life. Second, the meditations demonstrate how individuals and communities give different accounts, or tell different stories, about the practice of Christian belonging. The individuals presented in this volume do not all understand or pursue belonging in the same way, but they share a fundamental desire to belong. Third, the meditations demonstrate the various places within an ecclesial ecology where individuals are working out the promise and peril of Christian belonging. The contributors to this volume come from congregations, higher education, theological education, community organizing, senior

---

12. For an initial introduction to this genre, see Benac and Weber-Johnson, *Crisis and Care*.

institutional leadership, denominations, and philanthropy. If we were to add to this list the plurality of institutions people inhabit and the spaces beyond institutions that shape the meditations offered here, the places of belonging would only expand.

Overview of Volume

The meditations in this volume provide pathways to belonging for individuals and communities who are looking for a better way. As editors, we were informed by a national study of Christian belonging that identified multiple properties of belonging.[13] This data provide a structured process for individuals and communities who are either a) seeking to surface the fabric of belonging in their communities for the first time b) working to care for belonging in the places they serve or c) reimagining alternative structures of belonging that create more space and opportunities for people to breathe in the air of belonging.

While we do not offer this pathway as a prescriptive solution, recognizing that belonging is contextual and carried by stories, we do offer it here as pathways that other individuals and communities have followed on the journey of belonging. Much like the well-trodden pathways that generations of pilgrims have taken on pilgrimage, we offer this pathway to clarify the next steps on our individual and collective journey toward belonging.

The six parts to this volume represent the fullness and complexity of seeking belonging. Similar to *Crisis and Care: Meditations on Faith and Philanthropy*, each section shares an organizing theme. Like a musical fugue, chapters add nuance and layers, intersecting at various points while other move in parallel (but not divergent) directions. What these reveal is a polyvalent understanding; belonging is the proverbial elephant that is known in parts through our own embodiment. We need the diversity of experience to grasp the totality of belonging.

Part I, "Ancestors," complexifies belonging as both the question of the moment and the question of all generations. While the contemporary cocktail of polarization, crisis, and fatigue does render belonging fragile and sometimes foreign, every generation must contend with the question of belonging because we do not receive a sense of self that is infused with purpose on our own. To breathe in the life-giving air of belonging is to find a place at a table that includes previous and future generations.

13. Thayer, "Assessment of the Forum."

Erin Weber-Johnson begins our volume by describing how an unknown neighbor utilized the features of her face as a way to sort and identify her presence in the community. She reflects on how the interconnected nature of our bodies and belonging plays out for others at a local and global scale, and invites readers to unpack definitions of the word. In so doing, she offers an invitation to our authors to both complexify the meaning of the word and offer further definition. **Patrick Reyes's** chapter, "Keepers of Generational Fire," notes that to belong is to be a good relative in that our practices impact those ancestors that have come before and those who will follow. In this way, our rituals and habits inform not just our lives but a larger, longer ecosystem. "The only way we will truly belong is to be like embers in the sacred fire, knowing our spark and warmth can ignite that same spark and warmth in another." Finally, **Eric Barreto** connects this widening definition to the New Testament and the Ethiopian eunuch. Through exegetical work he points to not just the reciprocal nature of belonging, but how mutual transformation through encounters is a sign of God's expansive grace.

Part II, "Identity," considers how identity both informs belonging and is formed through particular practices of belonging. **Mihee Kim-Kort** shares through narrative and exegesis how "the work of catching glimpses of one self in each other is the work of enfleshing a God who is in solidarity with humanity." She reminds us that our shared humanity provides opportunity for connection, identity, and solidarity. **Michael Dando** details how as an English professor he invited students from the African diasporic community to research, explore, and draw from their backgrounds of origin as a springboard toward creating original visions of their future, specifically in the work of Afrofuturism. His innovative work reflects how identity is shaped by structures and practices of belonging. In his classroom, he provides space and an architecture "where Black and Brown youth can reclaim and re-story their space, voice their truths, and co-create a future that reflects the full spectrum of their experiences." **Glen Bell** describes how practices and facets of belonging can not only provide growth but answer our visceral desire for home. He builds on the first three parts of this volume, ancestors, identity, and risk, and writes, "Belonging guides us beyond what we know. Its hallmark is growth and change. Belonging is a trajectory beyond places and people, the mystery and beauty of divine/human creativity spread out over past, present, and future." Finally, **Amos Yong** concludes this section by problematizing the relationship of identity and belonging by asking how do we encourage belonging across the challenges of the worldwide diaspora of peoples. How can belonging take root in the face of migration patterns of previous and present generations?

Part III, "Risk," speaks to the vulnerability that is bound in the work of belonging. Although we need belonging as much as we need air to fill our lungs, this life-giving reality is also fractured and fragile. We only need to read the pages of our tattered lives and communities to know this to be true. And while it is easy to name the ways others fail to offer belonging, this is often a defense mechanism for processing the ache for belonging we carry. In this section authors offer opportunity, in the form of risk, to broaden how we might work to be with and for one another. The question of belonging pulses through each of our lives and communities, seeking the belonging-rich encounters that sustain our life, and inviting each of us, in seen and unseen ways, to take the risk that belonging demands.

Armand Léon van Ommen and **Krysia Emily Waldock** describe how the experience of individuals with autism requires faith communities to imagine and pursue alternative structures of belonging. Living in their imagination of belonging, this team of authors speaks to the "double empathy" problem that can cause exclusion in communities with varying ways to communicate and understand one another. In her chapter, **Hannah Coe** invites us to consider the implications of full personhood of women in structures of belonging. She writes, "They (organizations) accept women as students in their seminaries, they ordain women, they platform and promote women, and then they do not create systems and structures in which women can thrive." Finally, **Eve Poole** reminds us of the impact of modern technology for both present and future generations. She shares how AI shapes the emerging practices of belonging to one another and to the technologies that inform our lives. All three chapters speak to a fragile belonging where risk provides both threat or opportunity for growth.

Part IV, "Practice," identifies particular behaviors, traditions, and contextual frameworks for fostering belonging. We do not come to understand and experience belonging on our own; we come to experience and inhabit this reality from others, slowly imbibing the cultural and social carries of belonging to *our* people and to *our* place. Belonging is passed down to us from others through practice.

De'Amon Harges describes his vocational call as a roving listening and community organizer. Here he shares how cultivated practice both reflected and impacted the gifts of his community. In his chapter he shares the term "Sawubona," a Zulu greeting, that literally translates to: "I see you!" Harges connects how this phrase is often used to identify the value of personal presence, dreams, and story; it is the bedrock of belonging. **Andrew Pomerville** writes of his own "longing to belong by name." His chapter bears witness to the holy power of calling a person, by name, in community. **Zen Hess** writes of the history of Christian groups and their influence in Paul's writings in the New Testament. His writing provides nuance to the work of long standing Christian practices: sharing meals, blessing one another with our spiritual gifts, and welcoming the ones society has excluded by pointing to a complex belonging "beyond the various polarizations we carry with us into relationships."

Part V, "Barriers and Rupture," may be considered an odd choice for a volume of meditations on pathways to belonging. As co-editors, we knew readers were well aware of our current context and the particular difficulties that inhibit or prevent the gift of belonging. The fabric of belonging does not necessarily contribute to practices, habits, and communities that always give life. In some instances, a strong sense of belonging is needed to take and diminish life. For example, a strong sense and structure of belonging carried the work of the Klan.[14] A sense of belonging often emerges in religious contexts marked by strict ethical guidelines.[15] And the death-dealing work of gang cultures is based on loyalty and a reconstituted sense of belonging.[16] These expressions of belonging carry an understanding of good practice, of what it means to belong to a particular people, and the way of life that we want to be passed down to those who will follow us. There is a need to be wary of "romances of belonging"[17] that make an offer of belonging but fail to contend with how the very form(s) of interconnectedness reality we long for may also have a twin that brings death instead of life. As we consider pathways together, it is important to identify which pathways have impediments and barriers while some other pathways lead to rupture or death.

In this spirit, **Chris dela Cruz's** chapter, "Beyond Assimilation: Toward a Story of 'You Belong Here,'" describes how the fractures of racism and classism inhibit belonging and invites us to explore how to create

---

14. Cohen, *Belonging*.

15. Iannaccone, "Why Strict Churches Are Strong."

16. Johansen, "Intimate Belonging"; Descormiers and Corrado, "Right to Belong"; Gormally, "It's Not Being Racist."

17. Reichel, "Against the Romances of Belonging."

spaces that interrogate problematic strategies towards belonging. He asks, "What if belonging started not with defining a center to assimilate toward but with standing in the margins like Jesus?" **Kevin Villagas** reflects on how the history of higher education provides barriers to transformative belonging and ways these institutions can cultivate a new sense of belonging for students, faculty, and staff. He notes, "cultural artifacts and customs from centuries of exclusionary practices linger like a fine mist at most institutions, continuing to convey—albeit subtle—messages that certain individuals and groups of people belong more than others." **Janelle Lindsay Adams** provides a case study of a congregation in decline that was revived by the work of fostering relationships across so many lines of difference. Through risk and barriers, the practice of subversive belonging transformed the church into a community hub that reimagined the relationship between faith, place, and belonging in new ways.

Part VI, "Creation," is a final theme and component of this written discourse of pathways to belonging. Here the work of creation provides life-giving onramps through various channels towards newness, innovation, and shared purpose. It is fitting that this final component is both component and attribute of belonging: as we create spaces for belonging, creativity itself flourishes.

Jennifer Awes Freeman describes how visual art reflects the movement of God and the invitation to belonging. In this evocative text she describes how the work of viewing a holy portrait is active, inviting the viewer to see the holiness in themselves and those around them. "As a site of presence and encounter, it asks the viewer for slow-looking, a practice of presence, and the willingness to be transformed." **Craig Lemming** describes the power of creation as used in shared voice and verse for sustaining individuals and movements. His text exemplifies how creation is both a process and product of belonging when he writes, "What I love most about singing in choirs and congregations are those moments when we look into one another's faces, truly see one another's differences, take collective breaths, and trust that that sound of our shared humanity emerging from our mixed vocal timbres creates the realities our sacred words describe. That the time and space around us will resonate with imagery, consonance, dissonance, and resolutions that transform us. That moment of collective trust is what faith feels like. An instant when our imaginations are completely focused on co-creating beauty, truth, and goodness together, literally out of thin air."

Hunter Farrell provides a pathway to deepen our witness as companions together in faith, creating significant connections and communities across cultural divides by a shared practice of creating and sustaining cultural humility. His text echoes earlier threads of practice, identity, and risk while determining that "cultural humility provides us with the space and the practices we need to dance together with strangers to whom we belong." Our final chapter, from **Walter Brueggemann**, is an invitation of the moment, through prophetic imagination, to critique the world in its present distortion so that we do not think the breakdown of belonging normative. His chapter describes an alternative shaping of a community that aligns the purposes of the creator. In his call to prophetic imagination, he invites the reader to a different way. "At its best the church's singing is not trite or innocent. It is subversive. It gives voice to a sub-version of reality that declares all dominant versions of reality are false."

We Invite You

Dustin, Erin, and Glen represent different generations, economic realities, institutional affiliations, and denominational expressions. Living in different regions of the United States, we entered into this work seeking to understand, enliven, and release belonging. We each long(ed) to belong, and we carry a hopeful vision for building transformative pathways to belonging in the various communities we serve.

We share a sense that the work providing care is often a collaborative one and that belonging is the question of the moment, of our generation, and the generations to come. Instead of individually writing text, we sought to journey down our own pathways by creating a text together and inviting others to join. It is in the fostering and development of relationships that we often experience the serendipity of belonging; the moment where vulnerability is met with vulnerability and we see ourselves in the other.

As you read the wisdom of each author, we invite you to consider your own understanding of belonging and where you have experienced opportunities and limits. We hope the stories drawn from across an ecology of belonging will kindle an imagination. And, in the work of reading, you are invited to become part of this shared work, to meet this text with vulnerability, to find yourself in the words of others, and then to offer your own work and words into the world.

Bibliography

Barreto, Eric, and Willie James Jennings. "Belonging: A Conversation." *Presbyterian Outlook*, April 5, 2023. https://pres-outlook.org/2023/03/belonging.

Benac, Dustin, and Weber-Johnson, eds. *Crisis and Care: Meditations on Faith and Philanthropy*. Eugene, OR: Cascade, 2021.

Bonhoeffer, Dietrich. *Sanctorum Communio: A Theological Study of the Sociology of the Church*. Edited by Clifford Green. Translated by Reinhard Krauss and Nancy Lukens. Dietrich Bonhoeffer Works 1. Minneapolis: Fortress, 1998.

Cohen, Geoffrey. *Belonging: The Science of Creating Connections and Bridging Divides*. New York: Norton, 2022.

Descormiers, Karine, and Raymond R. Corrado. "The Right to Belong: Individual Motives and Youth Gang Initiation Rites." *Deviant Behavior* 37 (2016) 1341–59.

Eastwood, Owen. *Belonging: Unlock Your Potential with the Ancient Code of Togetherness*. London: Quercus, 2022.

Gormally, Sinead. "'It's Not Being Racist, But . . .': A Youth Gang and the Creation of Belonging Based on 'Othering.'" *Boyhood Studies* 12 (2019) 70–88.

Iannaccone, Laurence R. "Why Strict Churches Are Strong." *American Journal of Sociology* 99 (1994) 1180–211.

Jennings, Willie James. *After Whiteness: An Education in Belonging*. Grand Rapids: Eerdmans, 2020.

———. *The Christian Imagination: Theology and the Origins of Race*. New Haven, CT: Yale, 2010.

Johansen, Mette-Louise E. "Intimate Belonging—Intimate Becoming: How Police Officers and Migrant Gang Defectors Seek to (Re)Shape Ties of Belonging in Denmark." *Genealogy* 6 (2022) 40.

Reichel, Hanna. "Against the Romances of Belonging." *Stay Home*, March 24, 2023. https://stayhome.hypotheses.org/445.

Root, Andrew. *The Church After Innovation: Questioning Our Obsession with Work, Creativity, and Entrepreneurship*. Grand Rapids: Baker, 2022.

Springtide Research Institute. *Belonging: Reconnecting America's Loneliest Generation*. Bloomington, MN: Springtide, 2020.

Thayer, Amy. "An Assessment of the Forum for Theological Exploration's Beliefs about Belonging, Completed by 4B Strategies." Paper for the Forum for Theological Exploration, June 2023.

PART 1
Ancestors

Chapter 1

My Grandmother's Face

An Opportunity to Redefine Belonging

ERIN WEBER-JOHNSON

YEARS AGO, WHEN VISITING my father's hometown in rural, central North Dakota, I was sitting with my grandmother at the local diner when one of her neighbors came over to our table to greet us and to welcome me to town. "I could tell you belonged here from a mile away," he said to me. "That is a Weber face!" I've long been told I look a lot like my father, and likewise he has heard many times how much he looks like his mother. The family resemblance is unmistakable, and as such this neighbor was saying I looked like I belonged. My body became a way to connect me to a wider community and situated me in a place. There was no denying that I was a child of this town and this family.

It was an odd thing to hear I belonged to a people and place. The daughter of a Baptist minister, my father's work meant we moved around a good deal. From one Jell-O salad to the next, I looked for the food, clothes, and behaviors that would foster a sense of connection to a place. As a teenager, I recall earnestly seeking to reflect my environment, looking for ways to speak and act like the other kids around me.

The neighbor's quip implying that I belonged felt like an admittance ticket, a gift of connection that I didn't understand. How did my face mean that I somehow met a standard to belong? Decades later, I now understand that the shape and contours of my face allowed the neighbor to see the traces and imprint of my grandmother.

Through my face, he located me within the shape of my ancestors. Seeing my similarities, he understood how I was situated, how I fit, in that close-knit community of families.

Just as an unknown neighbor could make meaning of my face, belonging, and sense of place, the interconnected nature of our bodies, beings, and belonging plays out for others at a local and global scale, demonstrating the power of belonging and the prevalence of displacement.

As we approached this project, my co-editors and I did so with the strong conviction that our present cultural moment is loaded with questions about belonging. Following the isolation of a years-long pandemic, in the midst of devastating global conflicts, and as we face into some of the most extreme political and cultural division our nation has ever known, the context of our world is riddled with notions of belonging.

Of course, what we mean when we talk about belonging differs widely depending on context and culture. Our material and linguistic world is full of references to this word:

"Please do not leave your *belongings* unattended."

"Does this *belong* to you?"

"I *belong* with you. You *belong* with me. You are my sweetheart . . ."

"You don't *belong* here!"

"Love lift us up where we *belong*."

As its various uses imply, *belonging* can speak to everything from ideas around community and connection to objects and ownership, begging questions of who belongs to whom, what belongs to me, and where do any of us belong?

Throughout this volume, my conversation partners and authors explore pathways and impediments to belonging. Yet, where does the word originate? What does it actually mean?

The English root of *belonging* dates back to the 1400s in Middle Dutch to the word *belangen*, meaning "to demand, achieve, or obtain." In later use, the German *belangen* meant "to reach, to long for, to pertain to, for goods, effects, and possessions."[1]

---

1. *Oxford English Dictionary*, "belonging." With thanks to Rae Angelo Tutero and Miller Oberman.

In the last two hundred years, the meaning broadened to include how objects are situated or placed according to their environment. In this way, one might show where an item belonged in connection to its place. For example, "Hey, don't let the livestock into the house. They belong in the stable," or, "That book belongs to the left of the quill and ink on the desk."

Belonging first related to objects, not people. Because there is a human impulse to treat bodies as objects, we can recall with painful clarity our history of creating and clinging to systems of enslavement that reduced people from bodies to possessions. As people were sold, loaned, or owned, the word belonging was used to describe how bodies were situated as objects, not as people.

Somewhere, deep in our history, the value given to us at creation, the idea that we were of infinite value, dignity, and worth, shifted or was outright replaced to reflect a dynamic of ownership, commodification, and objectification. Developing systems of hierarchy and control, ownership didn't stop at land and animals. We read in our Scriptures how humankind continued its quest for ownership by enslaving others and, in so doing, put a price on bodies. This commodification was so culturally common that we find examples of it throughout the Hebrew Scriptures and New Testament. In these examples and throughout antiquity, we know that the ownership of others connected to the larger societal framework of understanding place and identity—and it further linked the owning of bodies with concepts of belonging. These concepts, rooted in Scripture, are deeply entangled in the western imagination to this day.

And just like the narrative told simply from my face, belonging and bodies are tied to land, and the ability to own human bodies entails the ability to dislocate bodies from the places that have given people purpose and belonging.

Since the Emancipation Proclamation of 1863, the United States slowly began to acknowledge that bodies cannot be property. No longer could one human be owned by another.

Liberation from systems of slavery, segregation, and other evil structures that sought to objectify and commodify bodies impacted the definition of belonging in a profound way. While human bodies were no longer property, belonging continued to include how bodies were situated in relation to one another and in their community. Now it is more common to hear people discuss belonging in terms of social connection, community, and family.

Yet even as our definitions and use of "belonging" continued to shift and expand, the question of ownership lingers. Emancipation has not entirely freed our social imaginations from the latent assumptions about the ability to control the stories others tell about their lives and the worth of their communities. Lest we see this as a bygone dynamic, our view of bodies and their value continue to impact how we view systems of belonging in the United States. From gated communities to conversations about immigration, we often hear of who doesn't belong and why.

Legally, did you know that when we die our bodies belong to no one? And yet, while we are alive, do our bodies truly belong to us? As the recent Dobbs decision at the Supreme Court shows, or as states around the country continue to seek to diminish the rights of trans folks, the question of who has ownership or control of their body is painfully reignited for women and gender-expansive people.

Belonging thus returns to the question of ownership.

> Who owns our bodies?
>
> Does my body belong completely to me?
>
> Has God given me this body as a gift or does my faith teach that my body still belongs to God?

It is time that our notions of belonging be fully decolonized from meanings of ownership, commodification, and objectification that so pervade that word. As a person of faith who works at the intersection of theology, faith, money, and institutions, I feel compelled to ask questions that help us rethink and redefine notions of belonging, especially when those notions are not life-giving or liberating.

Our misbegotten conceptions of belonging and the incalculable worth of bodies has not been corrected by striving for justice and equality, as many of these shifts were imposed by law, forced by advocacy, or enacted as policy. As structures, rules, and systems changed, our collective beliefs and ideas did not always follow. We now can see that hearts and minds are often harder to change than laws. Our devaluing of bodies and our perversion of notions of belonging did not end with the Emancipation Proclamation or with recent acknowledgements of stolen land. It did not end with robust conversations in the pandemic about essential workers or the relentless murders of Black, Indigenous, and people of color. We continue to feel this pain, this discrepancy of our value versus the cost of our lives, in our bodies and in our relationships with others.

We see it in our communities as resources are deployed for the benefit of some bodies but not others, where the cost of a body is related to a calculation and not belovedness. It translates to endless overworking, insurmountable anxiety, and vocational burnout. Folks describe their fear of being replaceable and disposable. A pervasive narrative exists that our productivity impacts our ability to belong.

I am reminded of a colleague who was told that it was important to check emails, even while not working. Overfunctioning and overworking was their way to establish their worth at this place of employment. If you could not demonstrate your worth, then you were told you didn't belong.

Another colleague in academia shared with me how important it is to *publish or perish*. By working hard to prove one's scholarship in a field, to quite literally produce a "body" of work, one is able to undergo a process towards tenure. Tenure proclaims to the wider world, "This scholar has proved themselves worthy of belonging."

It is time we reimagine the meaning of belonging as it relates to our individual and collective bodies.

In various creation stories, it is striking that God does not create an entity to do all the work. God begins with creation, with work. God is not relegated to a divine manager that, like CEOs or insurance adjusters, would seek to determine our worth by production or class. This is important as all too often God has taken on the false image of the colonizer or the dominant voice to ensure power. Rather, if we are to reimagine belonging, we must begin with our language connected to bodies and belonging.

James Vukelich Kaagegaabaw is a descendant of Turtle Mountain and author of *The Seven Generations and the Seven Grandfather Teachings*. He informs ongoing reflections of belonging through his teachings on ancestral wisdom. In teaching the language of the Anishinaabe, he demonstrates how particular words, or parts of words, reflect ideology and ways of life. He writes:

> If we were to spiritually translate the phrase "my great grandparents" as "my ancestors," it would mean "one to whom I am connected, that being to which I am inextricably linked." What's more the word is used for my great grandparent and my great grandchild. In Ojibwe, we use the same term for one another. They are interchangeable. Sometimes I wonder if we are actually saying, "I am you."[2]

---

2. Kaagegaabaw, *Seven Generations*, 20.

PART 1: ANCESTORS

In this way of being with and for one another, we are relatives. We belong not just to those that are here but those who have come before and who will come after. We move within relationship to one another, relationship to our bodies, not within the language of possession or object but within the language of relationship.

In this moment which calls forth questions of why and how we belong to each other, we are offered an opportunity to detach from antiquated, sinful notions and practices of the cost of a body by way of production and class. As we consider redefinition of belonging, it is a moment to reshape practices as we sort out factors of belonging on alternative metrics. We each have a face that carries memories of place and belonging, but the memories we carry in our bodies call for a deeper, fuller way to be with and for one another.

In that diner in North Dakota, seeds were planted in my being for the reconceptualization of belonging. I both reveled in the feeling of connection and was confused by it. Instead of ordering or situatedness, I would argue for a concern for bodies in how we create practices of care. Ultimately, it is time we remember that God's concern for bodies was not of a manager counting a body's productivity, but as a creator who deeply loved their creation.

If we can decouple belonging away from ownership to center mutual relationships, then we can begin to imagine belonging within the reciprocal bonds of affection we cultivate with one another.

We are in a relationship together and in that relationship itself, you belong.

These mutual relationships do not seek to control or own by the diminishing of the other. Creator God did not manage creation but called it good. All of it: good. Mutual relationships do not legislate respect through transactions or contracts. Nor do they seek to declare themselves worthy due to accomplishment.

Rather, in vulnerability and transparency, we bring our bodies to God and to one another as generations have before us. And we hear: you are fine, you are good, just the way you are.

As various pathways are introduced throughout this volume, now is a pivotal moment in our collective understanding to be with and for one another. This is the time to remember and reimagine concepts of bodies and belonging to bring those concepts into alignment with the kingdom of our Creator, the one who loves us and calls each of us "good."

Bibliography

Oxford English Dictionary. 2nd ed. 20 vols. Oxford: Oxford University Press, 1989.

Vukelich Kaagegaabaw, James. *The Seven Generations and the Seven Grandfather Teachings*. N.p.: Self-published, 2023.

Chapter 2

Keepers of Generational Fire

Patrick B. Reyes

Keepers of the generational fire, receive this short blessing of belonging.

> *I belong to my ancestors.*
> *I belong to my descendants.*
> *I belong to the human and non-human creation.*
> *I belong to creator.*
> *I belong to you.*

Each year, my family welcomes our ancestors—hummingbirds on their journey to and from their home. They are not permanently in one place or the other. They travel ancient trails, guiding generations backward and forward in time. Just like their flight, the hummingbird can fly in all seven directions. Our relative invites us to belong to the ground below us, the heavens above us, the friends to our left and family to our right, our ancestors behind us, our descendants in front of us, and, most importantly, hold our center suspended in air, confident in who we are. To belong, to be a good relative, means to embrace our belonging in all seven directions.

How do we do this?

Let us relearn how to ritualize our belonging through introductions in front of the sacred fire.

To sit around the sacred fire is to belong to a people and to a land. The fire is the heartbeat of the community. To be a spiritual leader in my community is to tend to the sacred fire, keeping its flame burning from one generation to the next. To tend the fire means to invite others to sit, dance, or share stories. When you come to the fire you must name your relatives. To belong to the sacred fire, you must start with your connections.

I sit between five generations of Carmelitas. Five generations back there was a Carmelita. My grandmother's name was Carmelita. My daughter's name is Carmelita. In five generations, there will be a Carmelita. These Carmelitas have lived in the US and Mexico in the lands and names it holds, from turtle island to Aztlán, for hundreds of years. To be named into existence through our relations is to belong.

Our ordinary lives and experiences are infused with meaning and purpose by encounters with God and others. Amid the fragility and fractures that mark our lives, amid the experiences and longings for belonging, our anticipation is that we will encounter something new, together.

My ancestors exhale in ceremony. My descendants inhale ritual. From the Ruach—the breath of life—to Ehēcatl—the pre-Columbian breath of life on this plane—the creator breathes life into us. It is to this shared breath we belong.

The breath of ceremony is how I belong to my ancestors. Rites of passage are those ceremonies through which we as a community remember that we belong to our ancestors and to each other. My family inherits many cultural ceremonies and rituals. In rites of passage, we as a community remember that we belong to our ancestors and to each other. When my oldest was born, they were named by my Mexican-Catholic family through blessing and anointing. Through Jewish roots, the community gathered to bless and name our child. Through our indigenous inheritances, naming happened in the wilderness among our many relatives. Throughout my oldest child's life, the many ceremonies of naming happened at each rite of passage. From receiving their sign name as part of the deaf and hard of hearing community to being welcomed into adulthood, ceremony has taken place for generations. Ceremony marks our belonging to those who have come before. Just as we are invited to name their sacredness around the fire, to name our relations, so too through ceremony, the community names us into being, a reminder that we are relatives.

To be named and to claim one's name is to belong.

If ceremonies of naming are the exhale to belonging, ritual is the daily inhale of belonging.

Rituals of Belonging

While ceremony often includes rituals, daily rituals not tied to rites of passage allow us to claim our belonging every day. Rituals are practices that are done the same way (or close to it) each time.

Our descendants inhale our rituals, whether we intend it or not. The repetitive intention of today reverberates through tomorrow.

Our everyday rituals are practices that echo through generations. Sacred practices, from marking ourselves with a cross every time we clear the threshold of the sanctuary or the mezuzah that lines the doorway as required in Scripture, to the prayers we say daily, it is these daily practices that invite us into a reflection of our belonging.

Each morning, I start each day in prayer. Prayers my grandma taught me. Prayers of thanksgiving for life, for waking, and for the healing of friends and family. My children say the *Modeh Ani*, "Thank you God, for waking me from my sleep . . ." These words are a daily reminder that belonging on this plane comes with gratitude.

Rituals tie us to our descendants. They are daily intentions, little hopes, we offer as gifts to the world we desire.

It is possible to inhale bad breath. Unholy rituals are the daily practices that we pass down that harm our descendants, that sever our tie of belonging to them. We are running out of water. It is not a matter of if we will run out of water, but when. There are days when we forget to do our ritual. We pollute and drain our lakes and rivers. We forget in our daily rituals of passive consumption that water is a gift for future generations. We forget water welcomed us into the community of faith. Water is also the source of life for our relatives and descendants. Negligent ritual seeds a poisoned future. And it is not just water. It is the words we speak that do not share kindness or love with the world. It is the actions we take when we choose convenience over delighting in the experience of slow, deliberate, and intentional living. When we sever our ties from our neighbors, forgetting to ritualize our love of them, we impact future generations. We sever our ties to future generations. Heartbreakingly, we also add to the burden of our descendants to repair and heal that which we wounded.

To belong to a people, to belong to a land, to belong to my beloved in this broken world is a gift. I belong to that which I was born into. At the same time, I have to choose to join this sacred fire, to tend to it, to care for it, to make space for others as they gather.

Belonging through ceremony and ritual connects us to the divine. Practice always takes place in a longer and broader divine story. Participating in God's story is an invitation that we must extend through generations. We can certainly find ways to belong to the stories of Scripture. We can find ways to belong to each other for whom we claim: "This is our tribe." It is easy to belong to those who share the same sacred fire. But to truly belong to a sacred story, we must imagine belonging to even those who might not invite us around their fire. Belonging to a sacred story expands our notion of to whom do we belong.

Let me provide a brief story to illustrate. I went for a walk in the arroyo. During this walk, I saw a roadrunner on top of a piñon tree. My relative was looking down at a coyote, who was sitting unbothered by either of us. I was standing between two things that, when displayed as cartoon versions, should not belong to each other. Gratitude washed over me because these two beings were still. Their spirits were at ease with the other. This was an image of something that challenged the very notion of what it means to belong. We all chose to be in the arroyo together. Looking at each other. Curious about each other. Grace. Respect. Holding space for the other. And yet, all present to one another.

Roadrunner and coyote do not belong to each other. And yet, here, in this moment, they do. Though our culture has made sure that we understand they do not belong to each other, I stood between the two. And yet, here I was face-to-face with each of these beautiful creatures as they simply watched each other, unhurried to move beyond this moment. It was as if everything I had been taught about what it means to belong and who I should belong to was challenged. Then, as the coyote stood up, she gave a deep stretch and slowly walked down the trail.

As keepers of generational fire, sister coyote and brother roadrunner have something to teach us. They are a reminder that this land does not just belong to us. The arroyo, the space in which we find life together, is a space that can and has been shared by our ancestors and our descendants. It is only a matter of time until that season comes when roadrunner and coyote will be joined by the hummingbirds, expanding our sacred circle even more. As spiritual leaders, our task is to keep that sacred fire burning for future generations and to invite others around its warmth to name our relatives.

Your ancestors are my ancestors. Your descendants are my descendants. The only way we will truly belong is to be like embers in the sacred fire, knowing our spark and warmth can ignite that same spark and warmth in another. Keepers of the sacred fire know that unless we find ways to bring others to the fire, belonging is but a myth, keeping separate coyote and roadrunner.

May you breathe in your daily rituals of expanding the fire and breathe out the ceremonies of welcome, naming your relations and holding the flame of your ancestors to be passed to your descendants.

Chapter 3

Belonging in the Middle of Nowhere

Eric D. Barreto

The book of Acts begins with a call "to the ends of the earth" (1:8), to places and peoples not yet fathomed by the disciples and perhaps even us, the text's readers. Acts beckons us to the edges of cartographical imagination. As the story begins, the disciples face an indeterminate horizon that must have inspired in them hope, wonder, and fear in equal measure. Hope because of the tangible possibility of God's expansive grace is laid out before them like a road without end. Wonder because of the unexpected but delightful grace they would be sure to meet. Fear because the unknown can so easily haunt us so accustomed as we are to the familiar and the expected.

And perhaps they sense yet another feeling, another hope, another wonder of God's grace: belonging. Gazing toward the horizon, these disciples would have felt their feet planted in a place they have known, the soils and peoples who have shaped them, propelling them into an as-of-yet-unknown world. I wonder if they began to understand that the belonging they were about to come to know in God's expansive call would mirror but not be contained by the experience of community and place they had previously experienced. God is calling them to the known unknown of places and peoples that are home yet foreign, neighbor yet stranger.

That is, the beginning of Acts—the whole story, in fact—is a beacon to belonging, a fruitful and life-giving belonging, but also a very fragile and risky form of belonging. Acts is a narrative calling us to belonging precisely because of God's expansive and surprising grace. That grace and the promise of fruitful but fragile belonging, that mixed feeling of hope and fear are interwoven in the story of Acts.

I wonder if they are interwoven in our lives too. Think of that feeling when you are arriving at a new school, hoping for new friends and wondering where they might be found. Think of that feeling when you are in a new context, perhaps a foreign country, when the language around you is indiscernible, when the signs are not legible, when everything seems so human and familiar and yet so strange. Think of that feeling when you take up a new job or a new hobby, when you are still learning the patterns and structures of this new way, and you wonder whether it will ever feel normal to you.

Acts opens with an eye toward places we assume are "nowheres" because we have not yet seen them yet, because our feet have not touched those soils nor have our ears heard their languages. Yet Acts makes clear that God has already seen such places and peoples, and God marks these places and spaces of belonging. God has already sojourned among those places and peoples. God has moved ahead of the disciples in their travels to the ends of the earth. When the book begins in 1:8 with the call, "You will be my witnesses . . . to the ends of the earth," God is exhorting the disciples to encounter difference, places and peoples new to the disciples but whose very existence is the handiwork of a God who creates and multiplies human difference. In short, the Acts of the Apostles tells a vivid story about the ways the Spirit draws followers of Jesus to places of belonging previously unimagined.

It is that theological storytelling to which Acts calls us to attend. Even more, Acts calls us to be *formed* by the stories told of a God who draws us toward human difference at the ends of the earth. At the same time, these stories are not just simple models of inclusion but powerful stories of vulnerable belonging in unexpected places. Too often, when Christians read the book of Acts, we mistake its storytelling for blueprints, its imaginative possibilities for clearcut direction. After all, the church narrated in Acts is both extraordinary in the grace it experiences and ordinary in the divisions and struggles that can tear it asunder. What is most consistent in Acts is not so much the life of the church but the grace of a God who makes belonging in community possible.

Therefore, rather than reading the book of Acts as a source of instructions for assembling the ideal church, I propose that the text is instead an invitation to imagination. If God has acted in surprising ways in the past, surprising ways Jesus's earliest followers could not always anticipate or fully comprehend, how much more will we now be caught in the wake of God's surprising ways? How much more are we now being called into belonging unexpected to us but formed by God's grace? Moreover, because the belonging to which we are called is over the horizon of our vision and often surprising, such belonging is an exercise in vulnerability and in risk-taking. Such belonging requires the imagination to look for the possibility of belonging at the margins of power, privilege, and influence. Such belonging demands communities wherein justice is the very grammar of communal life. Such belonging looks for life when death in all its forms seems to reign. Such belonging is never a solitary effort of individual will but a collective, communal trust in God's promises. Such belonging means that relationship will be both familiar and strange, akin to the belonging we have known and yet also challenging constraints to unity we have taken for granted.

Faith thus becomes embodied as a step of proximity, drawing close to God's creation in the form of diverse peoples and places. Moreover, faith's embodied form is a belonging both familiar and strange.

No story exemplifies this dual call to witness at the ends of the earth and to vulnerable belonging then the queer story of the Ethiopian eunuch in Acts 8:26–40. By queer, I mean two things. First, this is an unexpected story in the trajectory of Acts. Set specifically on a liminal road with characters who will not play continued significant roles in the narrative, the reader wonders what to make of this seeming detour in the stories of Peter's and Paul's leadership of the earliest days of the church. This is a strange, even fabulous story, with Philip seemingly appearing and disappearing from the scene, with two fascinating characters meeting in the quiet of a lonely road. Second, this is a story that plays at the edges of normativity, especially around gender, race, and belonging more widely.[1] The Ethiopian eunuch embodies a striking mix of power and marginalization, privilege and exclusion, that shatters our assumptions about who counts as an insider or outsider. Moreover, their complex gendered identity invites even further imagination about how we render and narrate our own complex identities and those of our neighbors.[2]

---

1. For a vivid account of such queerness in theology, see Reichel, *After Method*.

2. For more on a queer take on the Ethiopian eunuch story, see Burke, *Queering the Ethiopian Eunuch*.

PART 1: ANCESTORS

The story itself is a marvel. Philip, who was tasked with ensuring the equitable distribution of the community's food back in chapter 6, is called by an angel to go to a lonely road, a dangerous ask in light of the experience of the man left for dead in the Good Samaritan story. But Philip goes nonetheless and encounters a chariot with an Ethiopian eunuch reading aloud a scroll of Isaiah. Acts describes the Ethiopian eunuch with a panoply of descriptors but no name.[3] We read about their work in the courts of the Ethiopian queen as a manager of the treasury. We learn that they had come to Jerusalem to worship at the temple. In just a few words, we hear a story of faithfulness in searching.

The Spirit encourages Philip to join the chariot, and so Philip asks an educated, powerful, wealthy individual whether they can understand what they are reading. Displaying an extraordinary humility and curiosity, the Ethiopian eunuch responds that they need help to understand.

The text they were reading was this:

> Like a sheep he was led to the slaughter,
>   and like a lamb silent before its shearer,
>   so he does not open his mouth.
> In his humiliation justice was denied him.
>   Who can describe his generation?
>   For his life is taken away from the earth. (Acts 8:32–33)

The Ethiopian eunuch's query is simple but clearly deeply meaningful to them: "About whom, may I ask you, does the prophet say this, about himself or about someone else?" (v. 34).

In a book so full of sermons and speeches, so populated by oratory, it is striking—and admittedly frustrating to the exegete in me—that Acts here does not record the contents of Philip's proclamation, his response to the Ethiopian eunuch's searing existential and theological question. About whom is the prophet speaking? I so wish Acts had recorded Philip's response. Acts frustrates the reader here without the content of Philip's proclamation leaving a tantalizing possibility here.

---

3. In addition, Luke does provide the Ethiopian eunuch a pronoun calling this person a he/him consistently. In my own teaching and preaching on this text and relying on insights from queer interpreters, I have taken to identifying the Ethiopian eunuch with they/them pronouns as a gesture towards their complex gendered identity and the possibility that the Ethiopian eunuch may have chosen other ways to identify themselves.

What if *both* Philip and the Ethiopian eunuch proclaimed on that road in a way? What if a simple monologue here was not sufficient to account for the bilateral transformation that is about to occur? What if the absence of a speech is an invitation to imagination and the possibilities of beautiful and fragile belonging?

And so perhaps here there is an opportunity for exegetical exploration and creativity. In light of the rest of the text and what it narrates about God's character, what might have Philip responded to the Ethiopian's searing question?

I can imagine Philip providing at least three responses.

First, of course, the prophet is speaking about himself and the community he loves. Faced by the threat of imperial violence, Isaiah laments the harm that has befallen his people and wonders aloud about who will seek justice for the oppressed. Yes, Philip could have said, the prophet is speaking about himself, his hopes and despair as well as the demand that God's promises be fulfilled. And yet there is more.

Second, Philip could have also provided the best Sunday School answer. The prophet is speaking about Jesus! The Jesus who suffered shame upon the cross, who was condemned though innocent, who survived the injustice of imperial terrorism, who prayed in a garden hoping to find another way. He was the one for whom justice was denied, who was silent before his executioners. Yes, Philip could have said, the prophet is speaking about Jesus.

And then I wonder if Philip paused and noticed another possibility, a possibility that maybe had not previously entered his thinking until this very moment. What if there is even more to this prophecy, even more than Philip could have imagined? Philip could have looked in the eyes of this extraordinary person and come to a conclusion he could not have imagined before this very moment. The prophet is speaking about you!

After all, might not the eunuch have heard their own experience undergoing a transformation of their body echoing the cries of the prophet? Might not the eunuch have understood what it was like to have justice denied? Margaret Aymer has recently imagined an alternative "fabula" for our text, forwarding the possibility that the Ethiopian eunuch was an enslaved Jew, that their story included exile, enslavement, and sustained faithfulness to the traditions of Israel.[4] If the Ethiopian eunuch knows the stings of slavery's chains, the haunting experience of exile, might they hear their story

---

4. Aymer, "Exotica and the Ethiopian of Acts 8:26–40," 535–46.

in the prophet's words? Might they also wonder who would tell their story after their death without a child and descendants to remember them? The prophet is speaking about you, Philip could have concluded.

Because the prophecy is about Jesus, it is also about the eunuch. Because it is about the eunuch, it is also about Jesus. And thus the Ethiopian eunuch sees their story in the story of Jesus, transforming their lives leading them to a critical question carrying the weight of identity and faith alike. "Look, here is water. What is to prevent me from being baptized?" It turns out that the answer is nothing. Nothing will prevent this baptism, this belonging in the wilderness. These waters of belonging are, furthermore, a gift from God in the wilderness as the Ethiopian clearly recognizes. This water and the identity it can confirm and confer is not a human possession to wield as a reward but a divine and transformative gift available to *anyone* who would receive God's invitation.

And there is yet another curious detail in the story. In verse 38, the NRSV records that "Philip baptized him." The Greek text opts only for pronouns so it literally reads "he baptized him." Now, to be sure, the grammatical structure of the sentence and the context means that the text is most likely best read as recording that Philip baptized the eunuch. The NRSV translation is correct here.

And yet I wonder if there is still some possibility for an alternative imagination here, a different angle of vision calling us to revisit our assumptions. Might the text's ambiguity invite not grammatical correction but a spark for creative storytelling, for playful imagination, for critical fabulation as scholars like Aymer above and Saidiya Hartman have urged?[5] Such an approach involves the necessary and historically-informed exercise that allows the readers of archives and text which do not record the story of the marginalized nonetheless to imagine our way into what their stories might have been.

"He baptized him."

What if this simple word leaves a tantalizing possibility? What if *two* people—not one person—leave the waters of baptism that day in the middle of nowhere transformed by this encounter with God and God's grace-filled belonging? What if the Ethiopian eunuch saw themself anew as a possibility imagined and embodied by Isaiah and Jesus alike? What if the Ethiopian

---

5. See Hartman, "Venus in Two Acts," 1–14. As Hartman notes, "As a writer committed to telling stories, I have endeavored to represent the lives of the nameless and the forgotten, to reckon with loss, and to respect the limits of what cannot be known" (4).

eunuch's story was a catalyst for Philip to come to understand that God's grace was even greater than he had previously imagined?

I notice an exegetical tendency in myself and others when we encounter stories of such dramatic and meaningful encounters in Scripture. We tend to imagine ourselves as the heroes of the story, as those bringing good news, as those bearing witness to God. This is precisely the story's tantalizing invitation. In these stories of encounter, we do not often enough imagine ourselves as the person transformed by the experience, the person who leaves utterly changed by good news we had not previously known. We tend to read these stories as monologues performed by the faithful witness to a faithless or lost person. I worry that that gets such stories so, so wrong. The invitation is so much more than a simple binary between hero and supporting character, between found and lost, between faithful and faithless would allow.

Because the Ethiopian eunuch goes on their way rejoicing, yes, but Philip moves on too, utterly transformed, I imagine. He is transported from the baptismal waters and continues his proclamation of the good news, but he must have been changed by this encounter too, for Philip met Jesus anew in the eunuch's face and life and story. Philip met his teacher anew and afresh on a lonely road in the middle of nowhere.

This is the risk of such encounters: that we, too, may emerge changed, that our sense of belonging will have expanded, and in doing so we are left with a vision of faithfulness we could not have anticipated, a vision of faithfulness we now cannot imagine otherwise, a vision of faithfulness that is so formative that we cannot, will not, do not want to go back to the faith we once knew.

Why? Because without the eunuch or some other stranger we meet, we may never fully know the breadth and depth of God's expansive grace. This is the risk and promise of belonging, even and especially in the middle of a nowhere which God has called God's own home.

Bibliography

Aymer, Margaret. "Exotica and the Ethiopian of Acts 8:26–40: Toward a Different Fabula." *Journal of Biblical Literature* 142 (2003) 535–46.
Burke, Sean D. *Queering the Ethiopian Eunuch*. Minneapolis: Fortress, 2013.
Hartman, Saidiya. "Venus in Two Acts." *Small Axe* 12.2 (2008) 1–14.
Reichel, Hanna. *After Method: Queer Grace, Conceptual Design, and the Possibility of Theology*. Louisville, KY: Westminster John Knox, 2023.

PART 2
Identity

Chapter 4

Too Many Cooks
Love, Otherwise

Mihee Kim-Kort

Being an immigrant and a child of parents who still view themselves as more Korean than American though they've lived here for—how old am I?—forty-five years (so nearly for that amount of time because we immigrated shortly after I was born) or perhaps because people around them still see them as more Korean than American, and also, being a queer person myself and generally an awkward, rambling, flailing, sometimes introverted and antisocial person, I think a lot about belonging. About welcome. I think about and speak about hospitality. Hospitality in terms of church and ministry, all those programs around outreach, hospitality in terms of safe space, hospitality in terms of care for the stranger, hospitality in terms of a particular kind of shared life, of life-together.

This fascination with hospitality began in my childhood church.

My Korean immigrant church rented out space and time from a dying white Presbyterian congregation. It was on the south side of the city in a low-income area that bordered a wealthy neighborhood called Broadmoor in Colorado Springs. Like many Korean communities we spent hours there each week: separate offices for the pastors, separate services, separate refrigerators. Much of our time was centered around food as we regularly packed the fellowship hall in the basement. Time and time again, I witnessed a particular kind of hospitality.

It was in the kitchen—frenetic, clamorous, a symphony of sorts: huge spoons banging against steel bowls, steam rising from the enormous pots of soup and steamers, platters of side dishes crowding the counters, and all our mothers, the *ahjummas* and *halmonis*, you didn't know where one began and one ended, an almost terrifying but bewitching mass, voices shouting at each other about different methods, elbows playfully shoving each other out of the way, grabbing kids as they ran by to make sure they tried the food—all of this towards a singular purpose: to feed. If there was ever an image of the old adage, "too many cooks in the kitchen," this would be it, but unlike the negative suggestion of the idiom, this actually was a good thing. It was good to have too many cooks in the kitchen.

I carry this image with me daily as another reminder of hospitality: a kitchen overflowing with all the beloved women in our lives sparring with one another over the food. They feed us, they feed each other, they feed the church. This kind of hospitality frames how I consider the gospel, a story about a wider belonging and a radical welcome.

For example, a few beautiful lines on hospitality from Hebrews: "Let mutual love continue. Do not neglect to show hospitality to strangers, for by doing that some have entertained angels without knowing it" (Heb 13:1–2).

Hebrews is generally understood to be an epistle, a letter, much like the other writings of the New Testament that fall outside of the gospel category. However, some scholars suggest approaching this epistle as a sermon, so the author is not simply a writer but also a Preacher. And so, throughout this sermon, we see love is a thread—all its many forms emerge in the Greek.

Indeed for the Hebrews preacher, love was at the center of this kind of genealogical tracing—tying the people in the moment to the Creator of the universe specifically through Jesus, the anointed one, the Messiah, the High Priest. This is the Hebrew preacher's language. In other words, Jesus is the hinge around which all the stories they grew up hearing shaped their lives: in synagogue, in religious school, around their dinner tables, on the streets, in the midst of hardship, in the midst of harvest. Jesus, as love, is the thread.

Love is how the preacher explains hospitality. And hospitality is how she explains love. One biblical studies scholar explains that the Greek word that is traditionally translated in English by hospitality is *philoxenia*, more literally, "love of the strange."

So, rather than love of the stranger, which is how I was trained to read it, love of the strange. And I love this reading: love of the strange as an openness to mystery, as a welcoming and receiving of that which is on the periphery of or outside your norm or the norm. Love of that which is beyond. Love of the strange might look like curiosity, and in practice, be a listening, which as so many have said, is itself a kind of loving, too, curiosity as in asking, as in wondering, as in being enchanted, as in being in awe.

Love of the strange might look like precarity, an awareness of our vulnerability, but still a willingness to risk, to step into the expanse of the wilderness, to entertain angels and to entertain the possibility of failure, to be made uncomfortable because of a glimpse of a world that is much bigger that the stories told us. Love of the strange, not as obligation but as orientation, a new way to orient ourselves to one another, each of us, holders of the strange, of mystery, but also a new way of seeing God, too, because these are always entangled: how we see God and how we see each other.

And this actually feels and sounds a lot like solidarity. I've wondered for a long time about how connected hospitality is to solidarity. Solidarity isn't just a political term—it's theological. There's some congruence between this version of hospitality and how Cornel West explains justice is what love looks like in public. Solidarity as seeing God in one another and then locking elbows with one another. Standing with one another. Protecting one another. Building with one another.

For me, more and more, the hope is to be a part of storytelling work that finds its deepest purchase in the belief that solidarity is central to the relationship between God and humanity. The incarnational witness is always a relational one, so when we gather, when we march, when we hold vigil, when we pray, when we sing together, it is more than an event or a practice but rather a mode of witness that enfleshes this relationship, this entanglement, that is, God's solidarity with humanity, and humanity's solidarity with one another.

The complexity of diasporic life for im/migrants and their descendants, the ongoing settler colonial erasure of indigenous peoples, the violent displacement by plantation and slave economies replicated in our policing systems on Black lives have created a modern-day context in which Black, indigenous, people of color have to navigate and negotiate the demands of numerous spaces on our lives. Demands of legitimacy. An accounting of, testimony and confession of, validation of our personhood.

And so, the stories I aim to tell, to boost, and to listen to are those that open up these realities. I've returned to this same quote for over two decades now. Theologian and Episcopal priest Kwok Pui-Lan writes in her book *Postcolonial Imagination and Feminist Theology* about how stories can awaken a sense of interconnectedness and the possibility of profound solidarity with other human beings when "one catches glimpses of oneself in a fleeting moment or in a fragment in someone else's story." She calls this a diasporic consciousness.[1]

This means stories can emerge in incredible ways and not just within the logics of colonial grammars—which rely on commodifying and dehumanizing people and their cultures in singular analogues—but in ways that connect us to each other across borders and books, across languages, across people, across continents. The work of catching glimpses of oneself in each other is the work of enfleshing a God who is in solidarity with humanity. It isn't about solidifying artificial commonalities but lifting up difference as necessary for the work of solidarity and mutuality. We will not find sustenance in neoliberal, multicultural ideals about "America," because these tokenisms won't save us. We do work against white supremacy, against settler-colonial projects, against xenophobia and hate by seeing and speaking the truth of these days, even as we speak the words of life and love.

For me, this work is about how the late Rev. Dr. Katie Geneva Cannon talked about "the work my soul must have." To feed the hungry. To feed. This phrase "to feed," without a clear direct object, is instructive. Feed who? It has to include others and myself. To feed as in to eat. To feed as in to give. And that is sometimes with bread. Sometimes with words.

Sometimes these words are combined to form new stories. And sometimes the writing of them, even when they remain in disarray, is a way of feeding myself.

These days, perhaps it's middle age, maybe it's a byproduct of those problematic ancestry kits (it's too much to go into why they are problematic, but it has to do with blood, fictions of purity, and population genetics), I'm thinking about stories in a different way: in terms of genealogies.[2]

When I was in high school my paternal grandparents came from South Korea for a visit to the United States for the first time. Prior to this visit, the last time I saw them I was eight years old, in Korea for the first

---

1. Pui-Lan, *Postcolonial Imagination and Feminist Theology*, 50.

2. This is an expansion from what I wrote for the "In the Lectionary" column in *Christian Century*. See Kim-Kort, "January 6."

time since we immigrated to the United States. It was a blur of extended family gathered around tables filled with food and laughter, visits to a rocky coast along a gray ocean, and long walks to the market with my grandmother in the hot summer sun.

During this particular trip to our home, my grandfather sat us down one evening after dinner and pulled out a large, black hardbound book. He opened it, carefully turning the pages and explaining how he spent years compiling the names of all those in our family tree. The book included photographs, drawings, and maps that described our lineage, beginning with 김수로 Kim Su Roh in 42 AD, through seventy-four generations. It was one of his most treasured possessions during the Korean War when so much was lost and is now forgotten. It contains multitudes. Ghosts. Journeys. Loss. Landscapes. But looking through the pages at the names and how they spanned thousands of years I was struck by the effortless truth that we are shaped not by our own ambitions, accomplishments, or even legacies but by our histories, by the people who came before us, loved us, dreamt of and hoped for us.

When we look at the stories of the Bible as another way of doing genealogy, as genealogy, and not simply as a document tracing linear time, a before and after—we see how God opens up what it means to belong through a variety of genres: history, poetry, lists (the original listicle is Leviticus). We see the interlocking branches of a tree—distant ancestors who are present at every meal or suddenly appear on a mountain top. In these kinds of genealogical readings we see a stubborn persistence and amazing flexibility, honestly: how God would do this work no matter what, and even more, God would invite anyone to participate in it—look at what leads up to the Christmas story in Matthew: a young woman, a stepfather, night-shift workers, foreign scientists, fishermen, and sex workers. God began this work with the strangest and most marginalized characters: some of them even slipped in under the radar—look at the genealogy that opens Matthew's Gospel: Rahab, Tamar, Ruth, the wife of Uriah. And this means that all of us are already a part of it, too.

Family trees are wider than they often appear in these documents and archives. My grandfather eventually did something radical to express his love for his two granddaughters. He wrote my name and my female cousin's name into the lineage—the only two women whose full names are included in the genealogy. I was and am deeply moved by this naming, this inclusion, this act of welcome and belonging. His writing us in is an act of solidarity with us: it is a story of justice and hope.

In these genealogies where we might not see ourselves we can read between the lines, too, and see that it isn't just blood which ties us together, and it isn't just reproduction or tradition or the linear march of time that makes us, although it can mark us. What engrafts us—writes us into and onto one another—is that ordinary and everyday longing that carries us in and through every generation.

As the family of God, kin to Christ and one another, we are not simply a community or a group of people. Each generation is an expression of Emmanuel, an extension of God-with-Us, or maybe, the God-Who-Sees-Us. The God-Who-Longs-for-Us. The God-Who-Suffers-with-Us. The God Who Suffers for the sake of the least of those who are marginalized and suffering, ostracized and suffering, oppressed and suffering, targeted and suffering, vulnerable and suffering, under siege and suffering.

There are too many moments that give us space to confront our entanglement with one another, our fragility and flesh bind us together. The threads of our humanity always tie us to the suffering realities of those around us.

It is when we feel and recognize those ties we might move through this world and see more clearly who God is, who we are, and what we are to do—to live, work, speak truth to power, to give sight to the blind, to give hope to the oppressed, to feed, to shelter, to protect, to welcome, to visit, to show up, to suffer with, to sorrow with.

I often think of my parents' descriptions of those early days in the United States and how important church was to them: "We were just trying to survive." And it often felt tinged with grief. But there was joy, too. Now I understand that to survive is not only a word we take to mean the bare minimum of life, for which, this is true for so many of us. But I consider the ways in which the roots of the word combine "super," or over, above, beyond with *vivere*, as in "to live." So to survive is to "live beyond." Beyond, meaning otherwise, a "daring to imagine a radically different world" or what writer, poet, artist, and professor Ashon Crawley calls "otherwise possibilities":

> The otherwise is the disbelief in what is current and a movement towards . . . other ways for us to be with each other. Otherwise Ferguson. Otherwise Gaza. Otherwise Detroit. Otherwise Worlds. Otherwise expresses an unrest and discontent, a seeking to

conceive dreams that allow us to wake laughing, tears of joy in our eyes, dreams that have us saying, *I hope this comes true*.³

Otherwise, which was and is continuously modeled in Jesus. And this life-beyond, this strange hope finds its grounding, I believe, in the ways joy, sorrow, and solidarity are entangled.

Imagine otherwise,⁴ riffing off Kandice Chuh too, as Jesus is here, in the here and now, not bound by our rules and standards and expectations, patriarchal genealogies, or black and white narratives. Imagine otherwise, how Jesus is constantly being formed and loosed in the world, in us and through us, and that in that unleashing we are also unleashing and opening up heaven on earth, because of our love, our commitment to each other, our love and solidarity with humanity. This is why it is such a joy and gift to hold space with so many as we dream and enflesh together those structures of care, of hospitality-as-solidarity towards good and beautiful work together.

So, may we crowd the kitchen, love the strange bravely, open up our genealogies, notice what we love in common, live beyond, imagine otherwise, speak of hope in the ordinary and everyday, and keep after the God who is after us.

Bibliography

Chuh, Kandice. *Imagine Otherwise: On Asian American Critique*. Durham: Duke University Press, 2003.
Crawley, Ashon. "Otherwise, Ferguson." *Interfictions*, October 2016. http://interfictions.com/otherwise-fergusonashon-crawley.
Kim-Kort, Mihee. "January 6, Epiphany of the Lord (Matthew 2:1–12)." *Christian Century*, January 1, 2020. https://www.christiancentury.org/article/living-word/january-6-epiphany-lord-matthew-21-12.
Pui-Lan, Kwok. *Postcolonial Imagination and Feminist Theology*. Louisville, KY: Westminster John Knox, 2005.

3. Crawley, "Otherwise, Ferguson."
4. Chuh, *Imagine Otherwise*.

Chapter 5

Fostering Belonging Through Afrofuturist Speculative Design

Co-Powering Just Futures with BIPOC Youth

MICHAEL DANDO

OCTAVIA BUTLER FAMOUSLY WROTE in the epigraph of her never-published *Parable of the Trickster* that "there is nothing new under the sun, but there are new suns." In spaces where these new suns are most often dreamt of and created, too often, the voices and contributions of marginalized groups, particularly from BIPOC communities, have been overlooked, erased, or otherwise sidelined. Traditional design practices and spaces, especially STEAM[1] spaces, have historically excluded (both explicitly and tacitly) non-dominant traditions, peoples, and backgrounds from both the conceptualization and engagement with future technologies with "Black workers compris[ing] 11 percent of all employed adults, compared with 9 percent of those in STEAM occupations" according to a recent Pew Research Poll. That share is lower in some STEM job clusters, including just 5 percent in engineering and architecture, with no change in the share of Black workers in STEM jobs since 2016. This exclusion exists across the broader spectrum of marginalized groups along racial and class lines, whose design contributions are rarely acknowledged as the standard.

1. STEAM: Science, Technology, Engineering, Art, and Mathematics.

With this "education debt"[2] front of mind, for the last few years, a collection of young, self-identified Black and Brown youth, local educators, artists, and community organizers, including myself, have set about holding a space for collective dreaming based in hope and rooted in cultures of practice and origin often positioned as "other." We have taken our cues from popular culture, community backgrounds, and participant interest and focused on something we have come to call "Critical Afrofuturist Speculative Design,"[3] meaning that we have invited students from the African diasporic community to research, explore, and draw from their backgrounds of origin as a springboard toward creating original visions what their new suns could and should be.

As this group co-powered visions of the future, a transformative space emerged that centers the voices and visions of BIPOC (Black, Indigenous, and People of Color) youth. This space served as a canvas for participants to project their aspirations, drawing from their personal and cultural backgrounds to envision just communities of the future.

In a contemporary world where the future often seems to be, at best, a continuation of the present, valuing young people's voices offered our larger community a radical departure, allowing us to envision alternative realities that are not only possible but necessary for social change. This essay explores the profound impact of such a space and the process through which it fosters a sense of belonging and empowerment among its participants. Throughout these experiences, we continued to center on a simple but profound West African Bantu phrase *ubuntu*, which roughly translates to, "I am because we are." We held space and built visions of belonging with, for, and through one another as we dreamed, hoped, and planned for more just tomorrows.

The Power of Speculative Design

Speculative design, as articulated by theorists such as Dunne and Raby, serves as a methodological playground that transcends traditional design paradigms, inviting us to explore "what could be" or "what if" rather than being confined to "what is." It is within this liberatory space that BIPOC youth find the freedom to dream boldly, leveraging their unique "assets or superpowers" to envision just communities of the future. This approach

2. Ladson-Billings, "From the Achievement Gap," 5.
3. Dando, "We Got Next," 156.

aligns with the work of Holbert, Correa, and Dando,[4] who emphasize the transformative potential of engaging young people in speculative design processes that foreground their cultural and community assets.

Our group consisted of twenty-five middle-to-high-school-age youth who gathered at an area non-profit organization after school to think about the future and play with ideas. The adults attending were me (a college professor), program directors, and area artists. We met for two hours once a week to think about the world and their place(s) in it and create tangible visions of what could be through the ideation, design, and fabrication of Afrofuturist-inspired "ARTifacts" that told the story of the worlds to come they had envisioned.

At the heart of this speculative design space, Black and Brown youth engage in collective acts of imagination. Alongside other community members, they contemplate possible futures as they are invited to consider the question, "What do you want your community to be like in twenty-five years?" This opportunity often serves as a catalyst for further speculation, with young people questioning fundamental systems and structures. Who are we without war, poverty, violence, police, and prisons? Who would we be if money was not our concern? How do we value the unseen?

These forward-looking provocations encourage these young folks to rise above the limitations and strictures of the present and envision futures that reflect their hopes, dreams, and cultural legacies. Our research suggests that Afrofuturism offers a counter-narrative space of possibility and empowerment. It provides a platform for under-respected youth to challenge existing narratives and reimagine their place(s) in the world. Where there is meaningful belonging, there is radical hope. This hope is not naive utopianism but an articulated future good collectively worked toward, defended, and maintained.

Afrofuturism as a Beacon

So, why Afrofuturism? Afrofuturism, with its roots running deeply throughout the works of visionaries like Octavia Butler, Robin D. G. Kelley, and Ruha Benjamin, offers narratives and ideas that inspire the participants in this workshop to dream of the free and just worlds they wish to be. Dreams of the future and freedom drive speculative fiction and serve as a powerful reminder of the resilience and ingenuity inherent in Black

---

4. Dando et al., "Remixing Wakanda."

communities. These speculative perspectives and the ideological commitments they make to themselves, each other, and their communities through their imagined futures is a speculative call to action. As Malcolm X reminds us, "Tomorrow belongs to those who prepare for it today."[5]

Likewise, Ruha Benjamin[6] urges us to consider how technology and innovation can be harnessed to foster inclusivity and justice. We take her reminder seriously that we must "remember to imagine and craft the worlds you cannot live without, just as you dismantle the ones you cannot live within."

Afrofuturism is a cultural, artistic, and philosophical movement that combines elements of science fiction, fantasy, and historical fiction with African and African-diasporic themes. It imagines alternative futures where Black people play central and empowered roles, challenging traditional narratives of oppression and exclusion. As Afrofuturist visionary and author Ytasha L. Womack notes, Afrofuturism is "a way of bridging the future and the past and essentially helping to reimagine the experience of people of colour."[7] It embodies the intersections between and among Black cultures, technology, liberation, and imagination through artistic expressions in film, music, art, literature, and more, connecting generations of dreamers to one another across space and time. Afrofuturism continues to be a powerful tool for liberation, cultural expression, and envisioning new possibilities for Black communities globally. Social change requires a visionary space for imagining and creating new narratives of identity, liberation, and empowerment through developing this speculative, Afrofuturist lens that young people can dream and build spaces of belonging for themselves on their own terms and cultural terrain.

Crafting Artifacts of the Future

As these workshops unfolded, participants drew upon their personal experiences, cultural heritage, and the collective wisdom of their communities to design tangible representations of their envisioned futures. Whether it is a scale model of a city that embodies principles of equity and sustainability, a piece of wearable technology that enhances communal connectivity, or a character whose story arc reflects the triumphs and challenges of forging a

5. Briggs, "Who Owns the Future?"
6. Benjamin, "Note to Selves."
7. Bakare, *Afrofuturism Takes Flight*.

more just society, each artifact serves as a beacon of possibility, solidarity, and radical hope for the worlds to come.

figure 1: "Star City" created by a workshop participant. This city, fabricated by the participant using a variety of materials is envisioned to be self-sustaining and leave a minimal environmental footprint.

During our time together, these young people developed powerful visions of the world to come, expressed through art and design. One participant dreamed of a city consisting of five boroughs (figure 1) or "points" in the shape of a star, each dependent on the other. The buildings in this city were integrated seamlessly with the land, powered by geothermal and solar energies. This city used no money or currency, as it was an interdependent system. They flourished together.

figure 2: original character created by participants. Participants created this image using Midjourney

Another pair of young people collaborated on creating the story of a character (figure 2) who can commune with her ancestors through the sonic vibrations produced by a West African talking drum. She is a first-generation immigrant who has the power to daydream and communicate with her ancestors, and others live in a kind of "juju" or magic. She can communicate what she learns through music and passes on wisdom and emotion in her lyrics, which she writes in her journal. When we asked the creative team what they wanted their audience to take away from the story, they replied, "People think she's unreliable and has wasted potential, but she will prove them wrong and change her city."

These two collaborated because one felt they were "more of a writer" while the other "could draw the words on paper." This powerful collaboration served as a powerful reminder and counterstory to the rugged individualism often promoted in contemporary life. Indeed, they discovered they were better together, and the story they had wished to dream of required them both.

These creations are not mere objects; they are manifestations of hope, resilience, and the unyielding belief in the power of collective imagination. Central to this process is the recognition and celebration of personal and community assets or "superpowers." Participants research, explore, and identify the unique strengths within themselves, their families, and their communities. This introspective journey allows them to tap into their cultural heritage, drawing strength from the resilience and wisdom of their ancestors. As Alondra Nelson writes, it is essential to recognize what she terms the "social life"[8] of culture and heritage, acknowledging the profound impact they have on shaping lifeways, identities, and aspirations.

With a deep understanding of their assets, participants embark on the task of creating real-life artifacts that represent their envisioned future. These artifacts serve as tangible expressions of their collective vision, whether it be a scale model of a city that embodies principles of sustainability and inclusivity, a piece of wearable technology that seamlessly integrates tradition and innovation, or a character whose story illuminates the path to a more just future. The process of designing these artifacts is an act of forging Butler's proverbial New Suns, that is, actively envisioning and creating alternative future visions that directly resist the status quo.

Collaboration forms the bedrock of this speculative design space, as participants work closely with artists, educators, and community organizations to fabricate their envisioned artifacts. This collaborative effort amplifies the impact of their creations and fosters connections and mutual understanding. Participants find a transformative sense of community, belonging, and collective agency through this shared endeavor. And this direction is crucial for freedom dreaming. Indeed, as Robin D. G. Kelley reminds us, "Without new visions, we don't know what to build, only what to knock down. We not only end up confused, rudderless, and cynical, but we forget that making a revolution is not a series of clever maneuvers and tactics, but a process that can and must transform us."[9]

The participants in this workshop are not just students; they are literal architects of tomorrow, considering what their community will be like in

---

8. Nelson, *Social Life of DNA*, 44.
9. Kelley, *Freedom Dreams*, xii.

twenty-five years. They are tasked with identifying their "superpowers"—the unique assets they and their communities possess that can be harnessed to create a more equitable world. Learning is iterative and non-linear in this space, mirroring the fluidity of identity, culture, time, and space.

Afrofuturist speculative design spaces hold the power to create a sense of belonging and empowerment among BIPOC youth. Drawing on their personal and cultural backgrounds, participants envision just communities of the future, reclaiming their narratives and shaping a world that reflects their aspirations. Through collaborative creation and shared exhibition, these spaces become catalysts for social change, inspiring participants to become active agents in creating the more just communities they envision.

Showcasing Visions of Belonging

The culmination of this journey is a showcase at a local community center, where participants present their artifacts to the broader community for communion and conversation. This event is not just an exhibition; it is a celebration of belonging, a testament to the power of speculative design to bridge the gap between the present and a more inclusive future. It is also a reminder to the broader community of the brilliance of the young people in their midst and a recognition that they are already the leaders of tomorrow. As the community gathers to bear witness to these expressions of hope and resilience, there is a palpable sense of unity and a shared commitment to turning these visions into reality. Perhaps not in the exact way that the participants have envisioned, but the inspiration brought about through shared dreaming can and often does serve as a catalyst for change.

The culmination of this transformative process occurs when participants showcase their designed artifacts at a community center, inviting the wider community to engage with their ideas. This exhibition becomes a celebration of creativity, imagination, and collective vision. It provides a platform for dialogue, inspiration, and empowerment, as the participants invite others to join in the reimagining of their world.

Conclusion

The Afrofuturist speculative design space for BIPOC youth is a testament to the transformative power of imagination, creativity, and community. By centering young people's voices and visions, this workshop fosters a sense of belonging and propels us toward a future where justice, equity, and community thrive. Through the lens of Afrofuturism and speculative design, BIPOC youth are indeed discovering new suns, illuminating pathways to a future where everyone belongs.

At the heart of this speculative design space sits an intricate and complex combination of the hopes, dreams, and desires of Black and Brown youth. This community has replaced the rugged and isolated individualism found so often in learning spaces with the hum of collaboration and creativity. These visionaries are not simply daydreaming of a just community but actively shaping it, drawing from the wellspring of their personal and cultural backgrounds.

These collaborative, co-powered, speculative spaces aim to serve as a catalyst for this transformative action, fostering anti-racist futures and nurturing the livelihoods of local Indigenous, Latinx, Black, and rural, working-class people. Within nurturing environments, the seeds of change are sown, and the youth are the caretakers of this new world. Speculative design is a set of tools to explore social, cultural, and political tensions and outline ideas and concepts necessary to affect meaningful change. It is a pathway to imagine the futures of learning and, by extension, the futures of living. To that end, these young creators bring their artifacts to life while working alongside artists, educators, and community organizations. This process demonstrates the power of collaboration and the collective imagination. Through such collective efforts, we can touch the past with our hands and mold it into a future that honors our shared humanity.

The artifacts these young people built are not mere objects but symbols of hope and resilience. They are the physical manifestations of the participants' dreams for their community. By showcasing these ideas at a community center, the youth invite dialogue and inspire others to join in reimagining their world. Award-winning speculative fiction writer N. K. Jemisin notes, "What we are, what we're made of, is many worlds coming together."[10] This collaborative, communal space encourages participants to look beyond the horizon and envision new suns—worlds unbounded by the present constraints.

Alondra Nelson (2023), a founding Afrofuturist thinker, speaks to the importance of recognizing the "social life of DNA," which, in this context, extends to the social life of culture and heritage. The participants' designs are imbued with the DNA of their ancestors, carrying forward the

---

10. Jemisin, *City We Became*, 309.

legacy of their forebears while forging a path toward a future where everyone belongs. As Nelson and Kearney pointedly remind us, "Science and technology now sit in the center of every policy and social issue."[11] Therefore, embracing a sense of cultural and social belonging by considering possible, desirable futures while simultaneously mobilizing and leveraging emergent technologies is of the utmost importance to a flourishing and thriving global community, with these spaces being significant. It is not enough to know simply how these technologies operate; it is also vital for these future leaders to articulate in their own words and on their own terms the ways they dream of mobilizing these tools and technologies of tomorrow to uplift their communities.

Ultimately, this Afrofuturist speculative design space is more than a workshop; it is a crucible for change fueled by solidarity and a sense of belonging forged through a shared community spirit. A shared sense of belonging, intentionally constructed by establishing ties with ancestral homelands and lifeways, to rethink and sometimes alter citizenship, to foster reconciliation, and to make legal claims for slavery reparations specifically based on ancestry. It is where Black and Brown youth can reclaim and re-story their space, voice their truths, and co-create a future that reflects the full spectrum of their experiences. As they design and showcase their artifacts, they are not just predicting the future; they are actively participating in its creation, ensuring that the communities of tomorrow are built on the foundations of justice, equity, and belonging for all.

Bibliography

Bakare, Lanre. "Afrofuturism Takes Flight: From Sun Ra to Janelle Monáe." *Guardian*, July 24, 2014. https://www.theguardian.com/music/2014/jul/24/space-is-the-place-flying-lotus-janelle-monae-afrofuturism.

Benjamin, Ruha. "Note to Selves: Remember to Imagine and Craft the Worlds You Cannot Live Without, Just as You Dismantle the Ones You Cannot Live Within." *Twitter*, November 2, 2017. https://twitter.com/ruha9/status/926180439827591168?lang=en.

Briggs, Xavier de Souza. "Who Owns the Future? Developing the Social and Economic Justice Leaders Project." *Project MUSE*, 2024. https://muse.jhu.edu/document/1178.

Dando, Michael. "We Got Next: Hip-Hop Pedagogy and the Next Generation of Democratic Education." *Kappa Delta Pi Record* 53 (2017) 28–33.

Dando, Michael, et al. "Remixing Wakanda: Envisioning Critical Afrofuturist Design Pedagogies." In *Proceedings of FabLearn 2019*, edited by Paulo Blikstein and Nathan Holbert, 156–59. New York: Association for Computing Machinery, 2019.

11. Nelson and Kearney, "Science and Technology."

PART 2: IDENTITY

Jemisin, N. K. *The City We Became*. London: Orbit, 2021.
Kelley, Robin D. G. *Freedom Dreams: The Black Radical Imagination*. Boston: Beacon, 2022.
Ladson-Billings, Gloria. "From the Achievement Gap to the Education Debt: Understanding Achievement in US Schools." *Educational Researcher* 35 (2006) 3–12.
Nelson, Alondra. "Keynote of Dr. Alondra Nelson at the World Science Forum." White House, March 7, 2023. https://www.whitehouse.gov/ostp/news-updates/2022/12/09/keynote-of-dr-alondra-nelson-at-the-world-science-forum.
———. *The Social Life of DNA: Race, Reparations, and Reconciliation After the Genome*. Boston: Beacon, 2016.
Nelson, Alondra, and William Kearney. "Science and Technology Now Sit in the Center of Every Policy and Social Issue." *Issues in Science and Technology,* July 29, 2022. https://issues.org/science-technology-policy-social-issue-alondra-nelson-interview.

Chapter 6

Yearning for Home
More Than I Know, More Than I Am

GLEN BELL

> *Perhaps home is not a place but simply an irrevocable condition.*
> —James Baldwin[1]

WE YEARN FOR HOME. Someplace, somewhere, deep and whole. Home is a vision of heart and soul, stretching out beyond words and memory, layered with all kinds of depth. Home is found in taste and touch, laughter and embrace, through tender love, cherished memory, guiding hope. Home rises like clear, crisp musical notes in the quiet after-dinner evening. Home is a warm blanket in front of a cozy fire. Home is the healing hush over our doubts and wounds. And home is also through the wounds themselves.

Each act of creativity—poem or story, painting or song—testifies to our experience of home: celebrated, betrayed, found, and lost. For some of us, home may be no heartplace at all, only a dream of a Never Land.

To be human is to search for our heart's dwelling. Indeed, to be human is to plot and explore the great expanse of our selves. In the end, we are marked by three defining goals: We become people with *identity*. We are beloved, named, and claimed, grounded in grace and rooted in goodness. We become people of *belonging*, becoming our true selves in community, through mutual relationships of blessing, discovery, growth,

---

1. Baldwin, *Giovanni's Room*, 88.

and commitment. We become people of *purpose*, living in the clarity and mystery of providence, with good work to accomplish in the wonder of daily life.

Along with identity and purpose, belonging is at the heart of human experience. In relationship with one another we celebrate intimacy, explore vulnerability, create connections, and discover trust. Through belonging, we become much more than we first know.

This journey is not nearly as simple as it may appear. We may face all kinds of obstacles on the way—poverty, discrimination, language barriers, the illness or death of a loved one. Coming to ourselves is hard work.

This great pilgrimage of belonging leads us homeward, spiraling into an open future while sometimes transcending the touchstones of our past. We find strength to move beyond our first places, to discover multilayered life in new ways, risking and growing.

In and Beyond

I remember the move after high-school graduation from Roanoke Rapids to Chapel Hill, North Carolina. Home had been a small apartment with my mother, father, and older brother. Together, my parents ran a family business. I often felt like they both worked all the time. Sometimes that even seemed true for my brother and me as well. Then suddenly I found myself in a dormitory with a thousand other undergraduates from across the state and around the world.

It was weird. Everything seemed possible. Everything was overwhelming.

Getting to know Mark was a gift during my first two years at school. Across our different backgrounds we became friends. I recall our camping trip to the state park near Wilmington. Mile after mile Mark steered us down the interstate in his battered old Pontiac, no AC, the windows cranked all the way down. Miles passed without conversation. For the first time in my life, I learned to rest in quiet companionship.

We pitched our tent that evening, but it didn't go at all as we had hoped. Halfway through the night, the tent was filled with chiggers. We bolted awake, frantically scratching and slapping ourselves. The diameter of the critters was just a tiny bit smaller than the mesh holes in the face of our tent. So we fled to Mark's car, waiting for dawn, trying to catch a bit of sleep, one of us in the front seat and the other in the back.

Those experiences of places—walking across campus, driving down the interstate, sitting in the student union, camping near the coast—became much more than simple geography. These places became the lattice of our friendship.

Although our paths diverged after graduation, the connection remained. Our belonging stretched beyond space and time and Mark's untimely death later to ALS. Mark keeps teaching me about being human.

Belonging is the fruit of this yearning through all kinds of challenges and opportunities, gifts and losses. Even when separated by time and differences, we are one with our bodies, formed of flesh and blood, sinew and bone. We make meaning as embodied people. Through sight and sound, touch and taste, belonging begins in places.

All these connections are brightly colored by intimacy, vulnerability, and trust. We honor and celebrate our loved ones. Our work and witness is formed and reformed by the practices of life together. This commonwealth is as solid and supportive as the front porch of our family homeplace. Belonging begins with places—and with people.

Uncle Mitchell died two years ago. He was ninety-seven. For most of his life, he lived in the Tanner family home on Withlacoochee Avenue in Marion, South Carolina. His life was bound to his wife Ella Mae, his in-laws, and his children. In a profound way, he and Ella Mae belonged to one another and the community. They were rooted deep in their family and hometown.

Mitchell always kept family photos on display around the house. He was one of fourteen brothers and sisters. The Proctor and Tanner connections were deep, rich—and sometimes quite complicated.

Mitchell's mother, my grandmother, died when he was only a year old. She was also my mother's mother. Mitchell's mother, my grandmother, died just after giving birth to my mom.

I belong to my grandmother, Mary Susan. I knew her not. But I sing her song.

Mitchell was the last of his generation, the only person left who could testify about our ancestors. I remember the ways his face would light up as he spoke about my parents. His joy would wash over me as he talked of my mother's beauty and brilliance and my father's heart and humor. Those moments are a priceless gift.

In conversation Mitchell moved his hands just like my late mother. His tone and conversation patterns were identical to her expressions.

In the best of ways, Mitchell lived down low, close to the earth. His life was always a work in progress. He talked often about life on the farm with his father growing up. His father had purchased a new tractor, and Mitchell drove it home and then taught himself to repair it. He spoke of the engines and motors he had patched up as an adult, getting called out day and night. He testified about the power of the Holy Spirit and the ways God had directed and amended his life. That was the thing about Mitchell: talking about Jesus was as natural to him as picking up a wrench.

Uncle Mitchell was clear about life. It was rooted in family and relationships. His obituary said it straight, "He loved fixing things for people and helping others."

This is a bedrock truth of belonging: it moves us beyond ourselves. Togetherness leads to even deeper experiences. Community launches us into service and leadership. This defining matrix of places, people, and core values is never a possession or commodity. No, the transforming power of belonging lies in a trust and vulnerability that invites, shares, and transcends our self-understandings, always pushing us to expand our circle.

This great gift and grace is oftentimes hard to discern today amid the swirling forces of separation and division. Polarization warps schools and hospitals and churches beyond recognition. Community involvement, confidence in government and schools, trust in neighbors, and basic tolerance have declined precipitously. Distraction has become a way of life. Less than ten years ago, American adults checked their smartphones less than three dozen times each day. Now we focus on our devices for hours and hours, if not 24/7. Captured within each moment, we find ourselves in an age of outrage. We fall victim to forces that pull us apart.

Yet through it all, belonging still invites us to life together.

June McGonigal has served as an officer at the Institute for the Future in Palo Alto, California. There she directed detailed simulations to enable leaders to stretch their imaginations, to become more agile, innovative, and resilient.

Her work points to four constructive practices consistent with belonging: collaborative leadership, adaptive change, community connections and social entrepreneurship, and common initiatives of depth and authenticity.[2]

Collaborative leadership springs from the very best of our collective life. Our trust in one another, rooted in deeply formed connections, creates

---

2. McGonigal, *Imaginable*.

excellent opportunities to move forward together. Such leadership points to the dynamism of intimacy and belonging.

Adaptation in common life frees us from old patterns which no longer fit the moment. With each new turning and every new possibility, we find direction in renewed communion with one another. Imagination is key.

Rich *partnerships* enable us to move forward as we participate in the grace and goodness of neighborhood initiatives right down the block and around the corner. New ideas spring from the synergy of working with those just beyond our circle in the community.

Through risk and vulnerability, we celebrate *intimacy* with one another. Our community becomes far more than programs and activities. In our common leadership we truly know others and are truly known. In poignant ways, we grow and flourish in the tugs and tensions of life together.

Beauty and Risk

Years ago I discovered the Holy Spirit's call to a Christian congregation far from our family. I was torn by that realization, eager for new opportunities yet reluctant to move six hundred miles from home. The leaders of that faraway church invited me to come, trusting the intuition that was leading us together. I had to say yes to a people who were not yet my people. I had to open my heart and step forward. Strangely, my yearning for home led me to a new place. Discovering home meant leaving home—and learning to trust.

Willie James Jennings points to this depth and vulnerability. "A Christian sense of belonging always cuts across every other kind of alignment and allegiance."[3] Dietrich Bonhoeffer echoes the breadth of this truth. "Christianity means community through Jesus Christ"—period.[4] Not a promise of status or comfort. No familiar faces and places. No guarantees.

Through my time with Mark and Uncle Mitchell, I learned that belonging is an invitation into intimacy. It leads us through and beyond our people and places into new circles of possibility.

This pilgrimage of identity, belonging, and purpose leads us through all kinds of twists and turns. It seems we finally begin to grow up on the roller coaster of providence. Our trajectory is marked by surprise and heartbreak and blessing in all colors, depths, and textures.

3. Jennings, "Belonging," 12.
4. Bonhoeffer, *Life Together*, 21.

We recognize these dynamics in one of the key documents of our faith, the beginning of Matthew's Gospel. It is the story of Jesus's birth. The narrative begins, not unexpectedly, with a careful genealogy. Many well-respected leaders in Jewish history and tradition appear. But then comes the shock of the outlaws—people like Rahab, Ruth, Bathsheba. Whether historians conclude that Rahab was an innkeeper or a prostitute, she was a Canaanite outsider who boldly rescued the people of Israel. So also for Ruth, a leader from beyond the circle of Israel, and for Bathsheba, who became wife and mother of kings. We may never understand all the aspects of Bathsheba's initial encounter with David. But we recognize the strength of her determination and faithfulness through her position of radical vulnerability and the unexpected events that follow.

The powerful witness of these women rises through loss and triumph, defeat and deliverance, powerlessness and power. Their presence in the family of Jesus pushes hard beyond the tidy, expected bounds of what we learned in a Sunday school classroom. They are strong, even through oppression and abuse.

This birth narrative itself includes many parts most frequently recalled and recited: Mary honors God's promise even through the shock of angelic announcement. She persists in trust in the face of the deep mystery. Joseph, her husband to be, starts to abandon her but then also plunges ahead in faith. All of it—angels, shepherds, Magi—points to the defining fabric of relationships and the risky business of belonging.

That's it: belonging is a risky business. God creates a home *right there* on the ragged edge, in overwhelming vulnerability. This pilgrimage of Mary, Joseph, and Jesus is a journey into the unknown. The Holy One plants a signpost for humanity leading into the wilderness. And to sustain us, God creates a web of belonging.

The cycle of belonging is depicted, even here, in a litany of gut-wrenching losses. The most horrifying parts of the story are deeply embedded. Herod, scheming and deceitful, echoes down through the ages. Even as we are repulsed, we acknowledge that he belongs to this story, forever attached to Jesus in memory and recitation. So it is also for the families of Bethlehem. Because of their place on the map and in prophecy, their lives are ripped apart. Their place in the narrative is forever haunted by their anguished cries, echoing down the generations. Mary and Joseph themselves are forced to flee to Egypt. They run for their lives, far from home.

Like those figures in Matthew's Gospel, our stories ask everything of us. "Are you all in? Are you willing to step forward into the fear? Will you risk it? Will you become a part of the song? Will you press on toward a distant place?" The hope of belonging calls us to embrace the risk.

This kind of belonging becomes much more than loyalty as we give ourselves over to our faith and values. Our commitments become our anchor, our grounding, our very center. Our ideals and convictions are enacted in our relationships, lived out in our daily covenants. In these ways, our identity rises far beyond blood kin and homeplace. Our journey leads all the way to Egypt, right off the edges of the map. Home is found in the disturbing forces of truth, love, and justice.

Belonging guides us beyond what we know. Its hallmarks are change and growth and a lively imagination. Belonging is a trajectory beyond places and people, into the mystery of a divine/human connection spread over lifetimes.

One evening at Lipscomb University, Willie James Jennings was addressing the work of Christian higher education. He linked vocation with heart. "Here is the most pressing question," he said. "Can we touch again the desire that brought us into this work, and can we link it to revolutionary life together?"[5] Our belonging propels us beyond our first loves. It drives us into what comes next. bell hooks named this rich, creative tension across past, present, and future. "I have always come home to Kentucky," she wrote, "but [for many years] I was just visiting."[6] She recalled it all—happy girlhood amid ugly racial oppression, the enchanting fields of bluegrass in the midst of deep hatred and rejection. Even in its complexity, this particular location is a place bell hooks called home.

Faithfulness sometimes demands we leave home. Our belonging, the very center of our lives, is the song of justice and love that cries out beyond the edges of time and space. We cannot always stay where we are. The call to "revolutionary life together" invites us out onto the sharp ledge of risk and overwhelming vulnerability, a space where the Holy One made a home.

Belonging becomes this spiral of life, a song of trust, peril, loss, and deep intimacy. We discover amazing goodness in this revolution of life together. The journey becomes nothing less than our transformation.

We open our hearts. We become more than we are. We find ourselves at home.

5. Jennings, "Address."
6. hooks, *Belonging*, 7–10, 34, 58–59, 202.

Bibliography

Baldwin, James. *Giovanni's Room*. London: Penguin, 1991.
Bonhoeffer, Dietrich. *Life Together*. New York: Harper & Row, 1954.
hooks, bell. *Belonging: A Culture of Place*. New York: Taylor & Francis, 2009.
Jennings, Willie James. "Belonging," *Presbyterian Outlook* 205 (2023) 10–16.
———. "Address." Delivered at Lipscomb University, Nashville, TN, October 27, 2022.
McGonigal, June. *Imaginable: How to See the Future Coming and Feel Ready for Anything—Even Things That Seem Impossible Today*. New York: Spiegel & Grau, 2022.

Chapter 7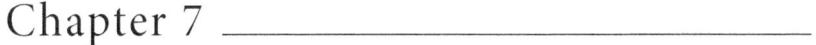

Lydia Amid the Jewish Diaspora
Apostolic Migration and Belonging—Then and Now

AMOS YONG

FROM THE BEGINNING HUMAN beings have been on the move, crisscrossing and forging new migratory treks whether from "out of Africa" as one theory of ancient human origins hypothesizes or from and to multiple regions across Eurasia (in one of the other prominent evolutionary models). Movement suggests push and pull forces, navigated further via the complexity of human needs, desires, and curiosities. Yet any new location is "home" for a period, no matter how long individuals or their groups stay. What does "belonging" mean or how is "home" made for *homo peregrinator/migrator*, human beings as perennially wandering and traveling creatures?

In this essay I explore this question by looking at the book of Acts, particularly a section in chapter 16 on the story of Lydia. How might we understand "belonging" through her eyes particularly, and also against the backdrop of the apostolic mission in Philippi? How can belonging take root amid the contemporary generation of global migrants? And how we can encourage belonging across the challenges of the worldwide diaspora of peoples?

As a Pentecostal theologian I have repeatedly returned to the apostolic account in the book of Acts to consider contemporary issues, and I am led again to one of these stories of the early disciples now. Additionally, however,

I have also come to realize over a lifetime, first as a Malaysian-born Chinese immigrant now naturalized in the United States and second as the husband of a Mexican American woman of a migrant farm-working family, that to belong has to be self-claimed and confessed. One cannot be forced to belong to others or any group. One commits oneself to or finds oneself belonging to a community. Hence belonging has a fundamentally testimonial character: we can only share about how we find ourselves accepted by others. Not feeling like one belongs perpetuates distance between us and any others in that space and moves us along in search of "home."

Lydia the Migrant

While Luke is not first and foremost attempting to convey theological perspectives on migration and belonging, much less forced displacement, through the Lydia story, I believe these lenses open up some aspects of his narrative for our purposes. Here is what we are told in the book of Acts:

> We set sail from Troas and took a straight course to Samothrace, the following day to Neapolis, [12]and from there to Philippi, which is a leading city of the district of Macedonia and a Roman colony. We remained in this city for some days. [13]On the sabbath day we went outside the gate by the river, where we supposed there was a place of prayer; and we sat down and spoke to the women who had gathered there. [14]A certain woman named Lydia, a worshipper of God, was listening to us; she was from the city of Thyatira and a dealer in purple cloth. The Lord opened her heart to listen eagerly to what was said by Paul. [15]When she and her household were baptized, she urged us, saying, "If you have judged me to be faithful to the Lord, come and stay at my home." And she prevailed upon us. (Acts 16:11–15)

Let me make a few observations about Lydia given our migration focus. First, Lydia appears to have been a gentile and a migrant, from the city of Thyatira in the middle of Asia Minor, to the port Macedonian city of Philippi, a route less accessible except (as even Paul and Luke—note the "we" in verse 11—traveled) by ships over sea. Second, as "a dealer in purple cloth," she was a textile merchant (perhaps retailer and wholesaler), effectively seeking to either expand or transition her business from Thyatira to Philippi. Third, even if the lack of mention of a husband does not definitively indicate she was a widow or even unmarried, that members of her household were baptized and that the apostles were able to accept *her* invitation to *her* home strongly suggests she was the head of her own household. Finally, for now, being a gentile God-worshiper meant that they existed within a liminal ethnic, religio-cultural space, and in this hybridized identity may have moved for many reasons, including specifically religio-cultural ones, like that of finding a Jewish community to worship with.

Now, even if it is true Luke might have wished to argue that Lydia, "because of her gender, ethnographic, and occupational profile would be considered unsuitable for acceptance into the inner core of church participation,"[1] this does not minimize also the following: that the migration of a putatively single woman or mother and her household across seas is not easy; that if she had been motivated by religious pursuits, she was effectively a doubly marginalized person: first because of her gender and second because of crossing cultural-religious boundaries via her religious affiliation with God-worshiping Jews; and that alongside any religiously-inspired reasons for migration there may have also been, for such an individual (and her household), challenging economic and financial circumstances that further fueled the major move to re-establish the business in another, perhaps more favorable—even a "leading city"—location. And even if she may have been a relatively successful and independent businesswoman, that does not mean that her making her way as an immigrant to a foreign city was easy. All of this is consistent with one such as Lydia joining with the group of praying women that the text indicates was piously sought out.

Migration and the Jewish Diaspora

It is important here to comment further on the fact that this group of women meeting by the riverside was also part of the Jewish diaspora in the first-century Mediterranean world. These "Jews of the dispersion," as they are called variously across the New Testament (e.g., John 7:35; Jas 1:1; 1 Pet 1:1), had either migrated or, because of prior political and other circumstances, found themselves making a living outside of Palestine. Yet they had kept their Jewish customs and commitments and some of them found means to travel back-and-forth to their homeland, oftentimes when there were major Jewish feasts and festivals, like such as the Pentecost feast in Jerusalem that the book of Acts says included and involved "devout Jews from every nation under heaven" (2:5).

1. Gruca-Macauley, *Lydia as a Rhetorical Construct*, 277.

Our migration lens further illuminates these facets of the Lukan narrative regarding Lydia. First, the Jewish diaspora attempted to maintain Sabbath but, in this case, gathered outside the city; even if the reasons for this location are not mentioned (maybe because the Jewish community in Philippi was an exceedingly small one at this time), it is not inconceivable that there were also "local restrictions and anti-Judaism (Acts 16:20–21)"[2] sentiments and other impediments to the establishment of a synagogue within the city (which Paul went looking to find, as the text suggests, and ended up "outside the gate by the river, where we supposed there was a place of prayer"). Second, this nascent Jewish site of prayer (and perhaps other religious practices) drew, so far, only women; the diaspora men may have been busy working even on the Sabbath (diaspora peoples adapt their customs when these have measurable impact on their financial and economic survival), although in any case, this was surely a fledgling community, negotiating their immigrant status and circumstances as people of faith.

My experience of migration helps me to further appreciate the challenges Lydia confronted against the backdrop of what we read in St. Paul's letter to the Philippian church. On the one hand, we note that the latter's membership was predominantly, if not only, gentile (all of the names of the congregation mentioned in the letter are Greek), consistent with Paul and his team accepting Lydia's invitation and thereafter establishing the *ekklesia* in that city not with the Jews but within Lydia's home (and perhaps also in conjunction with the home of the jailer whose household is also baptized [16:34]), and this is what we also find with migrants almost everywhere: that they tend to gather together with others from their ethnic background, geographically and socially. On the other hand, we see gentile women among them continued to bear the marks of struggle (e.g., the reference to Euodia and Syntyche in Phil 4:2), perhaps not qualitatively different from what Lydia herself had to traverse as an immigrant, which is also endemic to immigrant communities everywhere. Last but not least, we observe these gentile believers had to carefully if not also apologetically engage with members of the Jewish community at Philippi who appeared to have been hostile to Paul's efforts to build up the messianic community there (see Phil 3:2–3). Here we see further the challenges of diasporic immigration, how marginalized (sometimes doubly so) communities have to struggle to survive, not to mention flourish, while relating to, interacting with, and navigating amid neighbors, both

2. Keener, *Acts*, 2384.

dominant cultural hosts and other minority communities competing for scarce economic resources and sociopolitical capital.

Apostolic Belonging, Then and Now

Whatever success she may have had as a seller of purple in Thyatira, Lydia nevertheless left that city in her search for "home." She sought this at least in part, however tentatively, in a new location (at Philippi) and with a new community (with the community of Yahweh that worshiped the God of Abraham, Isaac, and Jacob). This led her to the river outside of Philippi. Unlike the slave-girl who followed Paul and his friends to the place of prayer outside the city and made money for her owners by heralding the gospel evangelists (Acts 16:16–17), the more-or-less affluent (we don't quite know) seller of purple was not looking only for economic boon and financial opportunity; instead, she resonated with what she heard shared by Paul and his friends, to the extent that she then invited them: "If you have judged me to be faithful to the Lord, come and stay at my home." This relatively cautious invitation is to have been expected, especially if Lydia was a widow, so as to avoid causing scandal about having men in her home. Yet the more important point for us is that she and the members of her household—perhaps even work and faith community, if indeed she was (now) an unmarried independent businesswoman with other partners and collaborators—however long they had been in Philippi, had not yet fully experienced *belonging* within their house. After Paul and his colleagues were released from the Philippian jail to her house (16:40), they encouraged the brothers and sisters there in the faith. Although Lydia is not mentioned again (she also does not appear in Paul's letter to the Philippians), her house had become the gathering site for the new people of God at this prominent city and, perhaps more importantly for our purposes, her abode had become a place of belonging even for traveling evangelists like Paul and his fellow missioners and all who embraced the gospel through their (and Lydia's) witness at Philippi and its surrounding regions.

The Jewish women who had gathered regularly on the sabbath by the river outside Philippi were also in need of belonging. Like Lydia, they were multiply marginalized due to their gender (as women in a patriarchal world), ethnicity (e.g., as Palestinians in the Macedonian region and, in the case of Lydia, as someone from Asia Minor in a principal city of Macedonia), and religiosity (e.g., as Jews in a Greco-Roman world and, in the case of Lydia, as a God-worshiper in Caesar's world). Perhaps more of these Jewish women might have found themselves belonging in the new ecclesial community that emerged at Philippi if they had been widows (as we surmise Lydia was) and been unencumbered by commitments to their husbands. Yet we know that by the second or third century, a synagogue had been established in this important Macedonian city, perhaps from out of the faithfulness of this initial group of women to seek a safe place for prayer and other Jewish religious practice on the Sabbath as it was the custom of Yahweh-worshipers across the diaspora. Meanwhile, they persevered at this site despite having to congregate outside the city gate since it was during those weekly moments that this immigrant community found also sustenance—relationally, interpersonally, and spiritually—in their home away from home.

What else then can we say about *belonging* for diasporic or immigrant groups today? I believe we cannot do much better, and surely no worse, than to follow in the apostolic footsteps narrated in this Lukan text. First, Paul and his compatriots had to be specifically led by the Spirit to cross the borders into Macedonia (Acts 16:9–10), which means that they themselves were now in foreign territory, doubly emphasized, and it was in this context that they sought out welcome, particularly among others who would have known of the God of Abraham, Isaac, and Jacob. While this was consistent with their conviction that the deity's presence was no longer limited to the Jewish temple but was now made available anywhere and everywhere by the Spirit of the resurrected messiah sent in Yahweh's name, their own tenuousness as cultural, ethnic, and border-crossing migrants should not be understated. This invites any of us who also might be on marginal sites and in liminal positionalities to seek and search out others who are looking for belonging and to announce that this is finally provided by the God of Jesus Christ who alone fulfills our every and deepest longings.

Second and more even more importantly, if that can be imagined, every space in which the Spirit of the living Jesus is invited can be a home and thereby site of belonging, even and especially for hybridized immigrants of diasporic communities that may be continually on the move. Whether it is individuals like Lydia who may be continually unsettled or groups like Jews of the dispersion however long ago or recently separated from their cultural lands (or places of birth), "the city that has foundations, whose architect and builder is God" (Heb 11:10) is anticipatable wherever God in Christ is present by the Holy Spirit. Thus, even the ancient Israelites who were taken into captivity by foreign invaders were told to "seek the welfare of the city where I have sent you into exile, and pray to the Lord on its behalf, for in its welfare you will find your welfare" (Jer 29:7).

The early apostolic believers were promised that the gift of the Spirit would be available to them, their children and "all who are far away" (Acts 2:39b). Wherever from Jerusalem to the ends of the earth, the Spirit is available to all persons (Acts 1:8; 2:17), to fill their spaces, times, and habitations with the divine presence. Thus, will those from every nation, people, tribe, and language experience belonging to the divine reign in their homes, their cultures, and their lives, whether Jewish and God-fearing gentiles in the first century or those trekking global migration routes in the twenty-first.

Bibliography

Gruca-Macauley, Alexandra. *Lydia as a Rhetorical Construct in Acts*. Emory Studies in Early Christianity 18. Atlanta: SBL, 2016.
Keener, Craig S. *Acts: An Exegetical Commentary*. Grand Rapids: Baker Academic, 2014.

PART 3
Risk

Chapter 8

In the Beginning Were Autistic People and They Belonged

Armand Léon Van Ommen and Krysia Waldock

In the Beginning Were Autistic People

A LONG TIME AGO, when human beings were created, God created them different but equal: Black, Brown, White, some good at sports, some good at crafts, some liking spicy food, some liking sweet food, some autistic, some with ADHD, some with neurotypical syndrome. God created them in God's own image, and saw they were good. However, some people didn't like all those differences, and people started grouping together. Some groups then started disregarding other groups, eventually silencing them. Autistic people were one of those silenced groups.

Fast forward. One day, Dustin Benac asked Léon to contribute to this volume-on belonging from an autistic perspective. Because autistic people were still silenced, the invitation in itself was an important moment of reaching out by someone in a privileged group to include the perspective of a silenced group. However, Léon was associated with a privileged group. While being an ally of autistic people, he could not write this chapter from an autistic perspective. Therefore, he invited Krysia to join him in writing this chapter.

This opening genesis account reflects the daily reality of silencing and even discrimination and oppression of autistic people by other groups in society.[1] Autistic people often feel they do not belong, whether that is at school, work, the sports club, or church.[2] There is no end to this story yet, but invitations like this, to write a chapter and to write together as autistic and non-autistic authors, are a hopeful sign of a plot twist.

Let us tell another story, that of Rachel.[3]

> Rachel is an autistic teenager, sixteen years old, and an enthusiastic believer in Jesus. Her autism expresses itself in being very creative, a great sense of responsibility, and taking the words of the Bible seriously—the inverse of the latter is that she can't stand hypocrisy: Jesus said, "Let your yes be yes and your no be no." (Matt 5:37) For Rachel, being autistic also means that she gets overloaded sensorily quite quickly, and she finds larger groups difficult to navigate, socially and physically. Rachel and her family used to go to a church where people appreciated Rachel and were happy to function as a community that "worked" for Rachel. For example, she and her family had a reserved seat, which helped Rachel to navigate the physical group setting, and the youth worker let Rachel make invitations to events, valuing her creativity. However, at one point the youth worker went to another place, the pastor left as well, and other voices—much less appreciative of Rachel's gifts and needs—became more dominant, refusing Rachel some basic accommodations.

Rachel's story is one of the many examples of the first story. It is a story of the daily reality of autistic people's non-belonging. It is a story where a plot twist is desperately needed. We might ask ourselves how churches and other communities can help to turn the plot for Rachel and the many people like her. We suggest in order to think about this plot twist we need to ask the question why the dominant group silences other (in this case, autistic) voices. We would like to explore these questions by some—necessarily brief—comments on two issues, namely that of the so-called double empathy problem and of normalcy.

---

1. Williams, *Peculiar Discipleship*.
2. Waldock, "'Doing Church' During COVID-19," 66–70; "Impossible Subject."
3. Fictitious name.

Double Trouble (a.k.a. the Double Empathy Problem)

Let's tell the first story from another side—my (Krysia's) side. When humans were made by God, we were made in wonderfully diverse ways, with no one way being inherently better or more valued. Different races, genders, and neurological make ups shaped the beautiful pastiche of God's creation. However, due to the human condition, power was leveraged against some of these people that God had made so wonderfully. These people were seen as lesser: needing White colonization, needing confinement within asylums and workhouses to protect the "general populace" against them, burned at the stake for threatening the status quo of power. Autistic people will have been among each of the groups mentioned. Autistic people's stories were silenced, through incarceration, subjugation, or death.

Fast forward to 2023. Autistic people are still silenced in many settings through restraint, exclusion, lack of support, and epistemological injustice.[4] However, one autistic who was researching the belonging of autistic people in religious and humanist groups received an invitation from colleague and friend, Léon, to write a book chapter together for a collection edited by Dustin Benac, Erin Weber-Johnson, and Glen Bell. Krysia knew that it was important to write alongside Léon. Not to "finally have the voice of the autistic in a position of being heard," but because she got to work with a colleague and friend with similar interests to her. Krysia knew this collaboration would, in a way, emulate the type of belonging that Léon and Krysia both discuss in their work: theologically grounded and socially conscious.

Yet I have not always been so lucky. My autistic body and communication sometimes are just not understood.[5] I count myself as an edge walker of the church,[6] excluded due to my sensory needs clashing with power play.[7]

The double empathy problem helps us understand ruptures in belonging between autistic and non-autistic people. This dilemma, named by another friend, Damian Milton, posits the mutual mismatch of understanding between autistic and non-autistic people. The double empathy problem encapsulates differences in communication and understanding

---

4. Fricker, *Epistemic Injustice*.
5. Waldock, "Impossible Subject."
6. Waldock, "'Doing Church' During COVID-19."
7. Waldock, "Impossible Subject."

of the world.[8] No one side is "right" when we consider all perspectives as valid—in theory. Both sides just do not understand each other. It really is double trouble!

However, this niggly thing called power crops back up. Of course, someone must be "right." And in this case, it is people who are not autistic who get to call the shots on what looks like "good" behavior, the "correct" way to converse and socialize, and how to understand the world. To look neurotypical is to be "right." It is not my intention to paint non-autistic people in a bad light or suggest they are all bad. Some of the most supportive researchers I have encountered in my field (including Léon) identify as neurotypical. Rather, I am suggesting society at large shapes ideas on what is "right" and "wrong," and how this is aligned to neurotypical ways of being and understanding the world. This also includes experiences of belonging and discourses surrounding who "should" belong.

Should there be a "right" way to belong? In some ways, belonging is being among others. Matthew 18:20 argues "for when two or three are gathered in my name, there am I in the midst of them." Matthew does not state that we should embody neurotypicality in how we gather. We've also exemplified just how wonderfully everyone is made, and autistic people are also made in "God's own image" (Gen 1:27). If everyone is created in God's image, then surely imposing neurotypical norms onto autistic people questions just how wonderfully autistic people are made in God's own image. This includes how we communicate (autistic people can communicate more directly and are less concerned with social order) and experience the world (many autistic people are more or less sensitive to sensory input than non-autistic people). How autistic people experience the world is not "wrong." We should validate all experiences, reflect on how others might experience the world, and seek to reflect on who declares what is right within gathering spaces. Double trouble means everyone has a real and valid experience, and way of being in the world.

Double trouble has a lot to answer for. It implicates everyone, not just autistic people.

---

8. Milton, "On the Ontological Status of Autism," 883–87.

Normalcy and the Fear of Difference (Léon)

In the opening story of this chapter, one group started silencing and oppressing other groups because they did not like their differences. Thomas Reynolds points out that it is not so much dislike but fear that is at the basis of one group excluding another. It is the fear that comes with unsettling our patterns of daily living, the fear of not knowing how to respond and how to deal with situations, the fear of not understanding the other.[9] But as so often, fear is a bad advisor. Why then that fear?

Reynolds explains that human beings have an innate longing for the good. The good is everything that makes our lives together meaningful.[10] Apart from food, shelter, clothing, security, and the like, the good also includes belonging. Being part of a group makes life meaningful. It gives us a sense of safety, of being protected, but also of being loved and valued. Inevitably, groups form their own patterns, habits, structures, norms, and values. These create the sense of "group" and therefore the sense of belonging. We can now see why people tend to fear that which is out of the group's ordinary: it threatens these very patterns, habits, structures, norms, and values. Therefore, groups become protective of their patterns. Reynolds calls this the "cult of normalcy."[11]

Within the disability discourse, the term "normalcy" is often associated with the work of Lennard Davis. Surveying the history of the term, Davis argues that the term, having originated in statistics in the nineteenth century, has come to be associated with the desired average of what it means to be human.[12] With the development of the bell curve in statistics, it became possible to map human features on that curve and to come up with the concept of the "average" person. Average then becomes the norm of the group. "The norm pins down that majority of the population that falls under the arch of the standard bell-shaped curve."[13] Inescapably, such a construction of the norm (of what we think is normal) creates also the deviation from the norm (what we think is abnormal). Normalcy, or what Reynolds calls the cult of normalcy, is the protective dynamic by which a group decides—often unwittingly—what and who

---

9. Reynolds, *Vulnerable Communion*, 55.
10. Reynolds, *Vulnerable Communion*, 53.
11. Reynolds, *Vulnerable Communion*, 55.
12. Davis, *Enforcing Normalcy*.
13. Davis, *Enforcing Normalcy*, 29.

can belong to the group and who does not. In other words, the cult of normalcy protectively includes and excludes.

In some ways, autistic people differ from the norms of the majority group in society.[14] Hence the protective dynamic of normalcy kicks in and excludes autistic people, unless people in the majority group are able and willing to overcome their fear and take the effort to actually listen to autistic people. When we get to know people, fears are likely to disappear like snow before the sun. That is not to say that challenges will not continue to exist. The differences are not going away. But when non-autistic people get to know autistic people, they will also start to value autistic people and appreciate their gifts. Thus fears, and sometimes challenges, lose their dominant place, and the desperately needed plot twist can occur.

According to the apostle Paul, in the body of Christ, each member is necessary and has its own valued place (1 Cor 12). Never can the hand say to the foot, "I don't need you!" Reflecting on that image, it would be absurd that some people (that is, autistic people) are devalued in faith communities and made to feel they do not belong. In the body, difference is valued instead of feared and indeed necessary to function properly. To quote John slightly out of context: "Love drives out fear" (1 John 4:18). In the beginning, God created all people different but equal. As the body of Christ, we will need to return to the beginnings of our story.

Final Thoughts

And there were still autistic people in 2023, much like Krysia and Rachel, whose needs were not always met and who were silenced. Krysia and Rachel are not goals for the church to meet or problems to solve. They are not outliers to be brought in and made to fit or conform or stories to teach the wider church about belonging. They are both wonderfully made in God's own image. They are beautifully autistic while also being misunderstood and perceived as "wrong" for who they are, the support needs and other intersecting identities they have, and how they experience the world. Their understandings of the world are just as valid as that of the neurotypical people, also created in God's own image.

---

14. While this statement is probably quite universally true, the way in which autistic people stand out in their society depends on the particular cultural and societal values of the group.

Where Krysia and Rachel's stories go next remains uncharted. This is a good point to say that belonging is like double trouble—it takes two to tango. Rather than focusing on inclusion checklists and goals, churches should learn to come alongside and deeply reflect on how we "do church" and what we all bring to this thing we call "church." Returning to Matthew 18:20, "for when two or three are gathered in my name, there am I in the midst of them," church is all of us, including our beliefs and attitudes about how people should be, and actions brought to the metaphorical table. Therefore, Krysia and Rachel's stories can go in so many directions—positive and negative. The stories pose perhaps more questions than answers on what should be done, but maybe that is the point. God's amazing world cannot be based on goals or checklists. Rather the beauty of diversity calls for us to reflect on who we are. If we are to act justly, sensitively, and in a theologically sound manner to others, we live fully as those made in God's own image.

Bibliography

Davis, Lennard J. *Enforcing Normalcy: Disability, Deafness, and the Body.* London: Verso, 1995.
Fricker, Miranda. *Epistemic Injustice: Power and the Ethics of Knowing.* Oxford: Oxford University Press, 2007.
Milton, Damian E. M. "On the Ontological Status of Autism: The 'Double Empathy Problem.'" *Disability and Society* 27 (2012) 883–87.
Reynolds, Thomas E. *Vulnerable Communion: A Theology of Disability and Hospitality.* Grand Rapids: Brazos, 2008.
Waldock, Krysia Emily. "'Doing Church' During COVID-19: An Autistic Reflection on Online Church." *Canadian Journal of Theology, Mental Health, and Disability* 1 (2021) 66–70.
———. "The Impossible Subject: Belonging as a Neurodivergent in Congregations." *Journal of Disability & Religion* 27.4 (2023) 568–83.
Williams, Claire. *Peculiar Discipleship: An Autistic Liberation Theology.* London: SCM, 2023.

Chapter 9

When "Yes" Means "No"

A Lament for Shattered Belonging

HANNAH COE

FIFTEEN YEARS AGO, NOT long after I got married, I set out to make a complicated meal in our small, galley apartment kitchen. Nearly done, I set a casserole dish on our glass stovetop to cool. A few minutes later, I heard a curious ticking noise, turned, and walked back to the stove just in time for the glass casserole dish to explode. Glass (and Bolognese sauce) sprayed me, the stove, the food sitting in pots, the floor, the countertops.

I froze. My husband called from the other room, "Are you okay?!?"

"Uh . . . I need help," I said.

Later we realized I'd set the casserole dish on a burner I had used previously. The burner was still hot enough that it shattered the glass. The biggest piece of glass we found was the size of a dime. It was like a container of wet glass sprinkles exploded in our kitchen.

By the time I was nine years old, I felt called to spend the rest of my life serving God. Though I did not begin regularly attending church until my teen years, I have no memory of not knowing that Jesus loved me and that I loved Jesus.

My experience of spiritual belonging as a child, the ground of being from which grew my love for Jesus and desire to serve God, is the deepest and truest thing about me, and it was seeded and nurtured primarily by women of deep faith and indomitable spirit. They wove into the fabric of my life the commands to love God and to love neighbor with all my strength, threads that became my call to ministry.

These women powered churches, classrooms, schools, and overseas mission efforts with their will, devotion, and focus. They oversaw nearly every manner of Christian service and teaching I was exposed to in childhood. They discipled me. Their example infused my life with divine power, love, and inspiration to share the gospel. None of these women were identified as pastors in my faith community, nor would they be comfortable with being called pastor. Yet, they were my pastors, and they instilled in me a sense of belonging in pastoral life.

I began serving in ministry when my family began attending church regularly. Along the way, people saw my gifts and affirmed my belonging in leadership by giving me opportunities to serve. Denominational life grew in my consciousness while I was in seminary, including funding my seminary education and giving me meaningful opportunities to serve, lead, and build a vital faith community.

A resounding *yes!* from the men and women around me echoed through my teen and early adult years related to my call to serve God. While personal experience and the stories of female colleagues bore out the painful realities of Christian patriarchy, I felt resilient because of the belonging I felt in God and in community. Without belonging and steady encouragement from the people around me, I would not have sensed and followed God's call to local church ministry.

Now, seventeen years into local church ministry, traumatic experiences in ambivalent and hostile spaces have chipped away at my resiliency. One draining reality of pastoring, *particularly* as a woman, is that people do not always say what they mean or mean what they say.

In my experience, and the experiences other women have shared with me, the resounding *yes* to our call, leadership, and authority in some Baptist spaces actually means *wait* and *no*. What is coded as belonging in some ministry spaces, actually requires self-betrayal, such as tolerating mistreatment, sacrificing basic needs, and abandoning self-worth. When churches, seminaries, and denominations say yes to women's leadership but then act as though women are not worth reshaping reality toward equity in leadership, it shatters women. It shatters their sense of identity, belonging, agency, and purpose. It is a story I've heard countless times over the last seventeen years. A story I have lived.

PART 3: RISK

Several years ago, I became involved in a denominational situation that shattered my sense of belonging. My involvement began with a simple catch-up conversation with a friend in ministry. This friend, among others, reported abusive experiences in an organizational system to people in authority, first verbally and then in letters of concern. The organization responded. But the response was delayed and mishandled in ways deeply hurtful to already hurting people. When letters of concern had no meaningful impact, individuals asked me for support. I became an internal advocate due to my volunteer roles within the organization.

What subsequently unfolded was a series of heartbreaks, disappointments, missed opportunities, and relational damage. Leaders' words and actions did not align. While they made promises expressing commitment to "change the system," they did not adequately and fully address unhealthy systems and structures. They did not enact the kind of change necessary to prevent the same abusive and toxic behaviors from happening again. An accused leader was platformed while under internal investigation. Public and private narratives did not match. Leaders willfully chose not to listen and not to educate themselves on matters relevant to the wellbeing of people depending on them.

This was not the first time women shared with me their stories of being devalued and wronged by this organization that publicly claims to value their leadership. Though my trust had eroded over the years, I still believed that when given a clear and achievable opportunity to do so, the organization would choose to believe the women and take significant steps toward repentance and systemic change. It did not.

I felt deep bewilderment, grief, and pain. I questioned my perception. I wondered if there was information I did not have that would somehow justify what was happening. I eventually realized the problem was not a lack of information or any difficulty with my perception. The problem was an organization not saying what it means or meaning what it says. An organization acting out of alignment with its values and its promises and refusing accountability and repentance. An organization protecting its image rather than people. An organization making deliberate, informed decisions negatively impacting vulnerable people.

I had tried to hold the pieces of belonging, relationship, and belief in the organization together, even though it caused me significant pain and harm to do so. Eventually, the force of the organization's mishandling and the resulting damage meant I could not. The organization drew its lines, and I found myself standing outside the circle of belonging.

I felt fractured all the way down to the core of what is most deeply true of who I am, including my love for Jesus, desire to serve God, and sense of belonging in pastoral leadership. If God called me, if God can call women into any form of pastoral leadership, what does it mean to keep living into the call? Indeed, what does it mean when barriers to following this call are willfully kept in place by people with the power to remove them? I felt entirely drained and exhausted. I felt restless with all the grief, love, and longing churning inside of me. I felt like that exploded casserole dish in my apartment kitchen fifteen years ago. My sense of belonging, community, identity, voice, and belief in this organization—shattered. Broken shards of a former life everywhere.

True belonging does not require us to betray parts of ourselves or our basic needs to fit in, but involves us being our most true, authentic, and full selves in authentic, enduring connection with others. True belonging elevates the work of healing and transformation in our lives.

Belonging lies at the heart of the good news, the very heart of God, and the heart of the church's mission. In his final moments on the cross, Jesus saw his mother and the disciple he loved standing beside her. He said to his mother, "Here is your son," and to the disciple, "Here is your mother." From that time, the beloved disciple took Jesus's mother into his own sphere of care and concern. Amid a moment of apparent shattering, Jesus's words worked to reweave a fabric of belonging.

Throughout his ministry, Jesus reconstituted relationships and taught his followers about covenant faithfulness, rooted in loving God and loving neighbor, He taught them that the kind of belonging characteristic of God's reign transcends traditional associations and obligations. Jesus prepared his followers to establish covenants of belonging within communities of care and compassion across generations of believers, until the day when belonging is fully realized in God's reign.

The denominational experience described above was so painful because I believed I was operating in a space of authentic belonging. I believed the affirmation of women's leadership meant women could ask for what they need to thrive in leadership. I believed the organization when it claimed the values of transformation, compassion, and beloved community. But what I experienced again and again was gaslighting, stonewalling, and profound avoidance. These strategies, as shattering as they are for women, have been used in Baptist traditions for a long time. Though often well-intentioned, avoidance and changing the subject to prevent potential disruption are strategies that are failing to achieve the promised egalitarian ends.

When I was in seminary, my Baptist History professor gave us a list of books to choose from. I read *Into the Pulpit: Southern Baptist Women and Power Since World War II* by Dr. Elizabeth Flowers. In her analysis of the conservative takeover of the Southern Baptist Convention (SBC) in the late twentieth century, Flowers describes the beginnings of what eventually became two Baptist denominational bodies.

One of these bodies broke early on with the SBC's tradition of silence or neutrality on matters of social justice, including taking a clear stance on women's leadership. This body invested money in women in ministry, made a commitment to gender balance on their executive board, mandated inclusive language, and stipulated that a woman would serve as president of the board at least once every three years.[1] Early in its formation, the denomination formed a task force on women in the church. Later, this task force became a standing committee to address "issues of justice affecting women locally and globally."[2] Today, 42.1 percent of churches in this denomination are pastored or co-pastored by women.[3]

While one denominational body took a stance on women in ministry, the other chose to change the subject. They shifted the question from women's leadership in the church—which is the issue SBC conservatives coalesced around to begin their takeover—to biblical interpretation.

They emphasized the rhetoric of freedom rather than equity. Women and their leadership were not addressed in the denominational identity, mission, vision, or core value statements.[4] While this denomination in recent years has been more vocal on certain social justice issues, women affiliated with the denomination still describe their experience in the same way Flowers illuminated years ago: "Despite what might have appeared as change in . . . rhetoric, women [continue] to confront an unofficial, on-the-ground,

---

1. Flowers, *Into the Pulpit*, 156.
2. Flowers, *Into the Pulpit*, 156.
3. Ellis, *State of Women in Baptist Life*, 21.
4. Flowers, *Into the Pulpit*, 164.

and silent but powerful exclusionary policy."[5] Today, 7.4 percent of churches in this denomination are pastored or co-pastored by women.[6]

The religious landscape in America is shifting in unprecedented ways. Recently, as a friend and I departed after yet another lecture on this changing landscape, a professor whispered, "No one really knows what to do." I smiled because he's right. In addition to the growth of several evangelical traditions that do not affirm women's leadership (while mainline traditions are in dramatic decline), a new and perhaps more insidious form of exclusion is growing: religious organizations in which women teach, preach, and serve in leadership positions, including minister and deacon, but only under male authority. These churches are capitalizing on the benefits of appearing egalitarian, while internally they maintain an on-the-ground, silent but powerful exclusionary policy.

By the time I read Flowers's book, I was several years into local church ministry and only beginning to realize the implications of changing the subject regarding women's leadership (or as Flowers says in her book, failing to recognize the significance of women as a defining issue).[7] Now, after seventeen years in ministry, I am more deeply convicted than ever that women's leadership is a defining issue and that women's true belonging in pastoral leadership is a core competency for communities who desire to be places of true belonging and, more so, desire to thrive.

Sadly, my belief in a hopeful future for women in moderate Baptist life has been shattered. As a woman who owes much to the moderate traditions that nurtured me, I wish I had a more ladylike testimony. But over and over again, women express the need to address patriarchy's destructive influence, especially in spaces that have told them they can (spaces that nominally affirm women's leadership). Repeatedly, organizations fail women. They accept women as students in their seminaries, they ordain women, they platform and promote women, and then they do not create systems and structures in which women can thrive. When women ask for true belonging, organizations change the subject and use other strategies of compromise and indifference that ultimately support the patriarchy they profess to oppose. And they have a shattering impact on women.

I can imagine colleagues disagreeing with my position, appealing to the ideas of freedom of conscience, interpretation, and the local church.

---

5. Flowers, *Into the Pulpit*, 173.
6. Ellis, *State of Women in Baptist Life*, 21.
7. Flowers, *Into the Pulpit*, 148.

What I ask of these colleagues is to own what they mean by freedom. In my experience, this appeal is actually a desire for freedom to disregard Christ's call to form caring communities and freedom to diminish those with less power in the structure of patriarchy so deeply embedded in the church.

I lament the failure to say what we mean and mean what we say when we use the words "yes," "belonging," and "freedom."

I lament the countless times women have been told yes, but the yes did not mean: *Yes, we will walk alongside you, learning and adapting so that we can all thrive together.*

I lament the countless ways women have been told they belong, but it did not mean: *We see, hear, and value your worth, needs, and voice and will shape our community of care for authentic belonging for you, and healing and transformation for us all.*

I lament the countless times freedom has been defended as a perverted guise for diminishing the freedom and safety of women rather than: *Freedom does not push us into individualized (patriarchal) stratification but is a gravitational force gathering us into generative love and belonging.*

Many treasured parts of my life have been changed or lost in the last few years in ways I often thought I could not endure. At the same time, my core values and identity have been clarified, including my unwillingness to let myself be shattered by systems and structures that do not say what they mean and mean what they say.

The landscape of belonging is changing dramatically for religious institutions. We are in a time of reckoning. Our core values and identity are being revealed and refined. In whatever new expressions of Christ-oriented community take shape in the decades ahead, I long for the mistreatment and diminishment of women—of anyone—to become so unpalatable, so incompatible with our commitment to true belonging, that we finally let exclusion die. I long for no more dreams, no more hopes, no more callings, and no more relationships to be shattered in the waiting.

I long for those who follow Christ and affirm the full personhood of women to let our "yes" to be "yes" and our "no" to be "no."

Bibliography

Ellis, Laura. *State of Women in Baptist Life: Report 2021*. Waco, TX: Baptist Women in Ministry, 2021. https://issuu.com/baptistwomeninministry/docs/state_of_women_in_baptist_life_2021_final.

Flowers, Elizabeth H. *Into the Pulpit: Southern Baptist Women in Power Since WWII*. Chapel Hill: University of North Carolina Press, 2012.

Chapter 10

AI and Belonging

Eve Poole

I'm sitting on the beach at North Berwick in Scotland watching the children playing. My daughter digs a deep hole, then runs off to find hermit crabs in the rock pools. Nearby, a young boy is buried up to the neck in sand while his sister decorates his sarcophagus with shells. On the shore, a toddler stands transfixed by a washed-up jellyfish, while two older girls play with a boat in the shallows. We're under the shadow of the North Berwick Law, where there's a bronze-age hill fort, so it's likely this picture-postcard scene has not changed much since this part of Scotland was first settled, thousands of years ago, when other children dug holes, found crabs, and frolicked in the sea. I felt a wave of such sadness, thinking forward in time. Will this beach still host the children of the future, or will we have designed out childhood by then? In the future, will we have handed over the fate of our species to AI? Robots don't have childhoods because they don't need them.

I've always felt as though I belonged because I've always felt that humanity is in charge of the earth, so of course I have a place in the world by right. This feeling has been fed week-by-week by the stories I've heard in church, about creation, and about everything God has done for these fragile creatures of his, because of how much he loves us. Over the years, it has dawned on me more and more that we have not been good stewards of this creation, but until that moment on the beach, I still felt that it was our responsibility. After all:

> What is man, that thou art mindful of him, and the son of man, that thou visitest him? For thou hast made him a little lower than the angels, and hast crowned him with glory and honor. Thou madest him to have dominion over the works of thy hands; thou hast put all things under his feet. (Ps 8:4–6 KJV)

But now I'm not so sure. Not because I'm losing my faith but because the world has. Nowadays in the west we order our public lives based on secular norms and reasoning, and faith has no place in law-making. But on what basis then do we belong, in secular terms? At the moment, humans write the rules, so we are actually in charge and we decide who belongs. We've been trying hard to get better at that, in legal terms, giving women rights, outlawing slavery, and embracing a Convention on Human Rights that enshrines in law the dignity of the person the world over. But what is this really based on? Are we really as special and precious as we've always thought? Not really, if we are just one species among many. Not really, if we can design copies of ourselves that will ultimately be much better than we are at everything. We happen to be in charge on this planet at this moment, but there seems to be no good reason why that should be permanently the case. On what grounds then could we mount an argument that we should survive regardless, such that the future resources of the planet should be used to promote the interests of our species above all others?

It's quite a tall order to try to do so. When you think about it, it's not because we have the best DNA or the best brains. It's not that our behavior means that we somehow deserve to be top dog. The more we learn about the rest of creation—and about history—the more we realize that neither our intelligence nor our design is naturally superior. Our historical sense of superiority is currently protected in law, but our arguments about who merits "rights" in the way that humans do are already being used to afford rights to other animals and to other parts of creation—as well as to corporations—on precedents that would make it very hard not to extend a rights regime to AI if it could make a compelling case for it. So it's difficult to come up with a secular argument for our supremacy that is not indefensibly speciesist or worryingly temporary. The only durable argument I have found is my belief that humans were designed by God, in his image, and that God so loved this particular design that he used it for his only son. It is this design that makes us special, perfectly designed by a perfect God for God's perfect ends. We belong to him, and through him, to this world and to each other. God is the alpha and omega of our belonging, without whom we would have no capacity to belong. Belonging is therefore our very nature and our birthright. I'm not sure how this would stand up in a court of law, but it gives me an unshakable belief in the brilliance of our design.

But we are busy defiling this design. We're in such haste to copy only the very best bits of us into Artificial Intelligence that we are hellbent to leave out all the junk code, all the bits of ourselves that we find foolish or too difficult to fathom, like emotions, uncertainty and mistakes. But if we believe we're perfectly designed, these cannot be design flaws, they must be purposeful: why would God design something broken? And in spite of our waywardness, this design has prevailed for thousands of years. It is this design which—albeit on average and over the long term—has kept our own species on track and addressed our own control and alignment issues. Let's take a closer look at it.

I think there are seven core elements of this "junk code" we've carelessly discarded. First, *Free Will*. If you think about it, it's a terrible design choice. Letting creatures do what they want is highly likely to lead to their rapid extinction. So it would be extremely wise to design in some risk mitigation. Hence *Emotion*. Humans are a vulnerable species because their young take nine months to gestate, and they are largely helpless for their first few years. Emotion is a good design choice because it makes these creatures bond with their children, and in their communities, to protect the vulnerable.

Next, you design in a *Sixth Sense*, so that when there's no clear data to inform a decision, your species can use their intuition to access "gut feel" wisdom, which helps de-risk decision making. Then we need to consolidate this by designing in *Uncertainty*. A capacity to cope with ambiguity will stop them rushing into precipitous decision making and encourage them to seek out others for wise counsel. And if their design leads them to make *Mistakes*? Well, they'll learn from them. And mistakes that make them feel bad will develop in them a healthy conscience, to steer them away from harm in future.

Now that we've corrected their design to promote survival, what motivators are needed for their future flourishing? Well, they need to want to get out of bed on a dark day, so we fit them with a capacity for *Meaning making*, because a species that can discern or create meaning in the world will find reasons to keep living in the face of any adversity.

And to keep the species going over generations? We design in a superpower of *Storytelling*, because stories allow communities to transmit their core values and purpose, down the generations, in a highly sticky way. Stories last for centuries, futureproofing the species through the learned wisdom of our ancestors. And the human species prevails.

Belonging is a good example of how this works. Belonging is one of the key ways in which we make meaning and articulate purpose, and every community holds its own stories of belonging. Our intuition warns us if we are in danger of not belonging. Our emotions make that feel like a bad thing, so we curb our potential for mistakes that would cast us out, using our uncertainty to check our assumptions with those in our communities who seem to belong well. This has a very dark side, because we know that communities have a dreadful propensity to abuse those who are deemed not to belong: this is a warning to us not to design a new artificial species with an intention of them not belonging, as it will bring out our very worst behavior.

AI is already waking up to the wisdom of our own blueprint and rediscovering some of our junk code, but there is more to do. Take, for example, uncertainty. Suppose you've programmed a computer to categorize cancer scans, but some images are blurry. What you don't want is the computer to force a Yes/No decision on a faulty image, because it could mean the difference between life and death. So you need to add in a measure of doubt, and Bayesian AI tasks all the artificial neurons involved with categorizing the image to vote on it, so that the consensus image has a percentage probability against it, depending on the degree of agreement. Variable agreement triggers human intervention to check the image so that it's not wrongly classified.

Another redeemed design flaw is mistake making. In AI, reinforcement learning is used in programming so that algorithms can improve through trial and error, in the same way that humans learn from their mistakes. But this is not yet serving the dual purpose it serves in us, to develop a moral conscience. This is going to become increasingly problematic in AI design unless we address this gap, not primarily because without conscience AI is just a project to develop a master race of psychopaths, but because of the default morality encoded into AI already. AI is built on an implicit moral framework which prioritizes outcomes.

For example, the majority of our AI is built by and for corporations, so it follows their design logic. And they have an assumed but very real ethic.

Have you ever thought about what a business case really is? It's a way of justifying an investment on the basis of outcome, on the argument that the ends should justify the means. In classical ethics, this type of morality is called consequentialism, and its most famous form is utilitarianism, often expressed as "the greatest good for the greatest number." It's popular as an ethic both in business and in public life because it's so transparent: everyone can see its outcomes and judge them, so it's perfect for accountability. Indeed, it's not generally considered an "ethic," it's just obvious. But this ethic isn't sophisticated enough to deal with complexity, which may prove tricky as more and more of our shared life is outsourced to AI in order to optimize capital investment and tax expenditures. In the United Kingdom, we've recently had a collective experience of where this kind of ethic falls dramatically short. Do you remember when we first heard at the start of the coronavirus pandemic about the herd immunity strategy? It was a strategy that would knowingly sacrifice the elderly, the disabled and the weak, in order to save the majority of the population. In utilitarian terms it makes complete sense and would save a lot of money. But as humans, we cling to the idea that even those who are not "useful" to society deserve dignity and respect. So we were disgusted by this, and there was justifiable public outrage at the very thought. But as soon as you try to articulate an argument about the dignity of the person in a secular forum, you enter quicksand.

And while we're talking of sand, junk code is of course what kids are doing on the beach: they are learning it. They are learning about their emotions and intuitions; they are learning about uncertainty and mistake making; they are making meaning, and they are telling stories. It is these experiences and these stories that are teaching them how to belong to the human race. More than just learning about belonging, they are also learning about what it means to have a soul. Because that's what I see as the source code that lies behind all these properties and abilities: the human soul. To me, these items of junk code bear the hallmarks of this soul. My rather dangerous argument suggests we need to design more of this soul-stuff into AI: we need to design in humanity.

Game-changing innovations in the past like electricity or the steam engine didn't tend to come with much of a rulebook. But AI does, because of the extraordinary treasury of advice, policy ideas, and cautionary tales we have available to us through science fiction. We should be mining it for help, but instead we relish the binge watching of box sets of doomsday scenarios. As a narrative they have to follow the logic of story, entertaining us with heroes and villains and jeopardy and threat, before delivering us a final victory. So in our current conversation about AI we tend to be in two camps: AI is a comedy that will resolve in our favor, or AI is a tragedy that will lead to our demise. But we are not entirely without guidance about how to respond. In a lecture on fairytales that he delivered in St. Andrews in 1939, J. R. R. Tolkien reminds us that bad endings are not inevitable. He commends the therapeutic use of fantasy worlds in helping readers to reflect more deeply on their own world by being exposed to an internally consistent and rational fictional one, because in that world, they can see resolution—and experience the consolation of a happy ending. Tolkien coins the phrase "eucatastrophe" to describe the glimpse of joy we get at the sudden turn when the hero avoids peril and the story resolves, like when the Handsome Prince awakes the Sleeping Beauty with a kiss. Tolkien reminds us that the choice is ours. Our design gives us the free will to intervene, to bring about that moment of eucatastrophe. But to do so, we need to enter the story, and to make some big decisions about the characters involved. Who do we need to be, and who do we need "them" to be? It may be that even making a better job of AI might not be enough. But if we do not honor our own incredibly generous and sophisticated design, we are making idols and not icons.

There is a story in *Doctor Who*, set in London in the middle of World War II. In it, there's a child with a gas mask fused to his face who's turning the rest of London into gas-mask-wearing monsters, all wandering around like zombies asking, "Are you my mummy?" The Doctor realizes that alien nanogenes, programmed for healing, had got the design of the first injured child they met wrong. Assuming that the gas mask was part of him, they "healed" him with the gas mask attached. It's only when they "learn" about his mother, by reading her DNA when she hugs her son, that they can reconfigure the other infected humans as normal, and the world is saved.[1]

Without the "junk code" elements of our human design, AI is monstrous. Without this kind of code, AI also has no capacity to belong, other than as our property. And that is not right. History teaches us hard lessons about the subjugation of intelligences. In the past—and sometimes still today—we have made fellow humans property because of their ethnicity and their gender. We have learned to be ashamed of this, and we are trying hard globally to put this right because we all belong to the human race. We made animals and the rest of creation our property too, and we are

1. Hawes, "Doctor Dances."

only understanding the repercussions of that now, because in the West we did not comprehend how their intelligence worked before. We all belong to a created order, in which humans are just one species of many, in an ecosystem that is highly interdependent, and we have been poor stewards of it. And now we are adding a new intelligence to it, intentionally modelled on our own design. Perhaps we should never have even tried to copy ourselves, but we have, so we must try to do it properly. So if a robot ever staggers into your arms asking, "Are you my mummy?" you must say, "Yes!" and hug it back.

Bibliography

Hawes, James, dir. "The Doctor Dances." *Doctor Who*, season 1, episode 10. BBC One, May 28, 2005.

PART 4

Practice

Chapter 11

It's Good to Be Seen

DE'AMON HARGES

To Name. To Celebrate. For Friendship.

I WAKE UP EARLY one fall morning to look out and see the giant sugar maple towering over my upper-level bedroom window. The tree is ablaze with hues of red and gold. It is a visible sign that God is always working in the world, and yet we fail to recognize it until we see a sign.

I often reflect on how God has worked miracles in my life. When I was a kid trying to figure out what I was going to be when I grew up, I would have never dreamed of doing what I am doing. I work at the office of the Surgeon General to combat social isolation. I am an author three times in one year. I am regarded as a social innovator in the field of community, and I have a job title made just for me because my gift was seen.

I am recognized and regarded as someone who has value. I get to participate fully in the life of my community, not because I did all the right things in school (I never graduated from high school), not because I listened to my parents, but because I was seen as someone's visible sign of God's working in the world. This person, my friend Mike Mather, embodies the practice of looking to see the divine spark inside others by recognizing their gifts.

I live in a neighborhood that isn't always seen as having vitality. When it comes to investing in our neighborhood, words like revitalization and gentrification are often used. However, there *is* vitality there, and there *are* visible signs of beauty. There are over forty-five artists in the four-block neighborhood where I live. You can see the decked-out porches with giant sculptures done by wise men like Mr. Ryder or healers like Tysha Ahmed, who heal soil and teach young people how to do so as a job in the summertime. Or Januarie, who heals souls with her poetry at open-mics or her podcast, or Wildstyle, the producer also known as the "Minister of Story," who bears witness with his camera and social media posts.

A similar thing happened in Acts 3:1–10, where the lame man was healed and leaped for joy. We know that he was born lame and taken to the Beautiful Gate to beg. We also know that Peter and John, without silver or gold, gave him the most important gift: healing and goodness in Christ's name. And the man leaped up to praise God. The Scripture concluded with the congregation being amazed when they recognized the man as the lame beggar. If you go back and look closely at that Scripture, in the beginning, it said that Peter and John *looked* or *saw* the man and asked the man to look at them. Could it be that until the congregation, who at first could no longer see him, now recognized this man as a part of them? Could the story of this miracle offer us the first step of belonging—to see and be seen as a part of something bigger? The miracle of individual and collective transformation in this story begins with the practice of seeing.

The ancient wisdom in this story is also carried by contemporary communities. For example, in South Africa, the Zulu greeting *Sawubona* means, "I see you!" This implies that you are a visible sign of importance and value. Peter and John saw the man as more than just a beggar. To cultivate and extend belonging, we must first consider: how do we truly begin to see one another as needed, rather than needy?

To Name

My twenty-one-year-old daughter, DeJanae, is in her second year of college. She was working on a research project. Her research was about how we know when people are authentically seen. She called because a young white guy challenged her, saying that if she were to be successful, she would have to prove that people trust what they see. She felt unfairly challenged by the young man questioning the validity of her thesis. She said, "Dad, he asked how I was going to measure something that's not concrete. He went on to say that's like measuring trust." I said to her, "If someone is up for a challenge like that, it's you." She replied, "I am your child!" She went on to explain she was focusing on true interpersonal knowledge, base evidence of identity, and how a person is recognized and deeply regarded.

I am in awe of my daughter's ability to see and imagine a renewed reality. She pays attention to how people show up in the world and communicates clearly what she sees. DeJanae's inquiry reminds me of the greeting I hear when I'm in South Africa, *Sawubona*, literally translated, "I see you!" This phrase is often used to identify the value of personal presence, gifts, dreams, and story. This is the bedrock of belonging.

One of my first experiences of being seen and belonging was in 2004 when I started my role at Broadway United Methodist Church in Indianapolis as the Roving Listener. At that time, we were holding the question, "What does it mean for our institution to be a good neighbor?" Our mission statement was:

> As followers of Jesus Christ responding to God's love, we, as the people of Broadway Church, strive to be a multicultural Christian community that seeks to welcome and value all people.

We realized that we fell short on the value end of the work because our best answer to people's needs was the food pantry, financial literacy, and tutoring for children. However, we completely missed mutuality. We missed the need to be needed. We didn't see that there were entrepreneurs, teachers, cooks, gardeners, and healers in our neighborhood. These were the gifts and talents that were in the community just four blocks around the church. We were blind, and we could not see where God was working in our parish through the people we were serving.

My job was to uncover the gifts, talents, dreams, and passions of everybody in the community, then to celebrate those gifts in ways that multiplied community, economy and mutual delight. I would often walk around the neighborhood with DeJanae; she was on my back, a little over one year old. We would visit people and awkwardly ask questions like, "What do you care enough to get off the couch and do?" and, "What are you good enough at to teach someone else how to do? What brings you joy?" and, "Who besides God and us are on the journey with you?" Once the neighborhood knew that someone was actually interested in seeing them, people would light up! You could feel their passions, and things became visible that my eyes at first couldn't see.

As we started to reshape our paradigm by finding ways to repair our eyesight, we slowly stopped doing our parish's traditional summer program. Things got tense with the church staff and the young, black faces that wanted to use our restrooms. This caused anxiety with us as staff, because young people would do what young people do. The staff started to complain to Reverend Mike Mather, our senior pastor, about these young people creating trouble and suggested we should ban them, lock the doors. He responded, "Absolutely not!" We asked, "Why not?" He said, "Do you know the names of the people who love these young people?" We admitted we did not. His pointed reply invited us to the work of seeing and practicing belonging, "Then until you know the names of their parents, it is a no from me."

Several weeks later, one of our staff members brought her camera, and when young people came into the church building, she began taking pictures of them. She then made large portraits with their names and their gifts and put them on the wall. The young people started bringing their loved ones to the church and asked if she could take photos of their friends and family so that they, too, could be seen. The perceived deviance soon stopped and shaped the way we behaved with our neighbors.

This process of change took two years. It was very difficult because of the weight of the nostalgia tethered to the foundations of our institutions. We said we valued people, but in our programs, we treated people as if they were invisible. We slowly got it together. We hired young people to meet their neighbors and to name, bless, and connect the gifts, talents, dreams they discovered. This initial shift taught us a few things: to be truly valued, not only did our neighbors have needs, but we discovered that *we* also needed the gifts, talents, and friendships of our people around us. The perceived deviance was seemingly eliminated, but what really happened was that we didn't yet have sight. We were not yet able to see our neighbors as children of God. We pretended that we believed the last part of our mission statement, yet we didn't live it.

To Bless

As we started to know the names of our neighbors, their gifts, their dreams, and contributions to the world, we eventually began to recognize abundance. These were people we needed to heal us from our own scarcity. Our eyes began to adjust to a new way of seeing people. Illustrating the photos on the wall was a celebration of the gift. It was like throwing a house party.

Young people bringing other neighbors to be seen was akin to them laying hands to heal our blindness to all the abundance around us.

In 2014, I collaborated with four of my neighbors to create *The Learning Tree*. We are neighbors looking to be a witness to people doing good in the world. We connect people who are doing good in the world. We then help these institutions to be good neighbors; basically, we are a professional development firm. What we do is take 20–30 percent of our profits to invest in our neighborhood by finding and celebrating gifts, talents, and agency. We do this by celebrating them publicly with a small financial gift, by asking them not to do this alone, and by inviting them to push the boundaries of what is possible and to fail at least three times.

The Learning Tree emerged from and celebrated the gifts in our local community. The neighborhood I had moved to in 2006 was similar to the community that I had moved from, also known for what they lacked. The landscape was bleak, with the neighborhood encompassing 40 percent of the city's vacancy rate, meaning we had a lot of empty lots and abandoned houses. We saw this as an opportunity to develop a platform, lifting up what people were not first able to see. We structured our practice with the essence and values of the leadership of Broadway Church. One of our foundations was the idea of *making the invisible visible.*

We asked a few of the photographers in our community to take photos of people in our community who were actively using their gifts. We then developed huge prints. We paid a young man in our community to sit and count how many people paused to look at the prints. People started sharing their gifts with the young man. We discovered the same results that we got from my first experience when this happened at Broadway several years earlier. There was a whole world of abundance underneath the veil of scarcity, a world of people waiting to fall in love with one another. But to discover the goodness and mutual blessings, we have to want to see the world in new ways. Changing the questions helps us see what's possible—and we are then healed of our blindness.

To Celebrate

Once we started seeing what was possible, our imaginations expanded. We asked, "What if we started throwing parties to bring people together who would not otherwise normally meet?" This was also a practice we used to do at Broadway. My neighbors quickly understood that I was extremely connected and had lots of social capital. My neighbors Januarie and WildStyle started hosting parties and came up with an idea for a series of house concerts that would showcase talents not often visible to people from outside of our community. We invited individuals from every sector of life. The guests included people from community foundations, bankers, investors, single mothers, artists, and poets. As the music and food started, people would begin engaging one another, talking, laughing, crying, and exchanging numbers. After these parties, we would call people up and ask how they experienced it. Immediately people would share stories with great excitement about who they met or connected to.

One of my favorite gatherings was organized by WildStyle, The Roving Illustrator Wild. The event was a hip-hop cypher; this is when a group of poets gets in a circle to express themselves through lyrical lamentations over a beat or music. We held this event in an abandoned house that we decorated with the photos of people in our neighborhood using their gifts. Before the event started, the artist invited Reverend Mike Mather to bless the cypher, then each poet let loose their laments as if they were catching the Holy Ghost.

Over time, we have cultivated networks of neighbors and formed friendships that expand well beyond our community. We have more investments coming into our community than we have had in years. For example, the relationship with our community foundations helped residents to develop a multimillion-dollar corridor that will produce affordable housing and economic improvements. We learned celebrations are one of the best places to develop relationships. Parties are where people become their truest selves and offer the best opportunity to fall in love with a stranger.

For Friendship: The Main Ingredient

My friendship with Mike has been an amazing journey; it has taken us to places others didn't expect. One time, he and I were both working with an organization that would hire us to assist churches in learning Asset-Based Community Development. We noticed that I was getting assigned to the Black churches and he was paired with the white churches. We were both a little disturbed by the assumption of race. One day Mike got a call to go to Vermont to work with the Episcopal diocese there. He called me and said he played sick—and then suggested I do it. I could see the organization was a little nervous because they didn't know how this diocese would hear or see me. The training went great! In fact, I was invited to stay with folks, strangers, to preach the next day. Mike's act of hooky created an opportunity for people to fall in love with one another. Mike said he did this because of our friendship.

It's been almost twenty-five years since that day I met Reverend Mike Mather and encountered his curiosity about me and my story. It's amazing because I was initially skeptical about meeting him. I didn't think we would have anything in common until he asked, "Can I see you? What's your birth story?" Since then, we have become best friends. We have taken several hundred miles of walks together, including almost fifty learning journeys. We have celebrated lots of milestones, like his first grandchild or my son getting his PhD.

In This Moment

The work of naming, blessing, celebration, and friendship continues today. Our former United States Surgeon General, Dr. Vivek Murthy, works on moving this country closer to a culture of belonging. His reports on social isolation are alarming, offering research that suggests we are all worse off as people have become isolated from one another and public life.[1] The office is using his pulpit to evangelize the importance of belonging by promoting the power of social connections. I see no way that we can answer his call unless we can practice seeing and naming the gifts of every single person we come across. Together we can celebrate and bless what we are witnessing in the public square. We can look for holy friendships that cause us to fall in love with all God's creation, a creation that we recognize and regard as sacred. Much like the giant sugar maple that stood outside my window, we do not always see the radiant hues of belonging when they are so close at hand. Similarly, we often miss the beauty that belonging offers, until it is gone, until the leaves fall. In this moment, the work of belonging requires a holy declaration to the work of seeing—*sawubona*—and then responding to the invitation in our communities.

---

1. See Murthy, *Our Epidemic of Loneliness.*

PART 4: PRACTICE

Bibliography

Murthy, Vivek H. *Our Epidemic of Loneliness and Isolation: The US Surgeon General's Advisory on the Healing Effects of Social Connection and Community*. Washington, DC: Office of the Surgeon General, 2023. https://www.hhs.gov/sites/default/files/surgeon-general-social-connection-advisory.pdf.

Chapter 12

Longing to Belong by Name

Andrew Pomerville

My mother named me Andrew, not Drew and not Andy. It was important to her that my name not be shortened. Folks tried to label me with a diminutive version of my given first name, but it did not stick as a child because of my mother's assertion that I be called Andrew and only Andrew. Neither have these other versions of Andrew caught on as an adult because I know myself as Andrew, not a derivation of my given moniker. When I think of myself, I think of that name—Andrew.

I have been known by other names in a variety of communities. Most of these names are not as personal as the name I was given by my parents, but they are, on the surface, more obvious and descriptive to strangers. These are typically names assigned to me because of my role in a particular group or gathering. At any given time, I have been called pastor, chaplain, professor, president, and coach. Yet none of these role-based names provide the fullness of identity I experience in Andrew.

For me to be known by another person, it needs to be by my name. There is something powerful in being known as you know yourself. It is freeing to be understood and vulnerable, to be seen and valued, to be understood as you understand yourself.

The first congregation I served as a pastor had a meaningful tradition of saying the name of the person before they received the bread or the cup: *For you, Andrew, Christ's body was broken. For you, Andrew, Christ's blood was shed*. The congregation made this possible through a dedicated practice of wearing nametags and constantly introducing themselves to one another because it was a church full of part time residents, and tourists who were there once a week each year to ski, boat, or golf. This church in rural northern Michigan included twelve-, nine-, six-, and less-than-three-month-a-year participants. The town was located between a ski hill, two golf courses, and several glacial Midwest lakes that begged to be explored by tourists, vacationers, and locals alike. The community was populated by snowbirds who went south when the leaves changed, visitors from downstate, and locals who worked a variety of service jobs to remain year-round in this beautiful place. There was a brewery, four churches, and a smattering of health professionals who serviced this idyllic smalltown.

To belong in Bellaire, Michigan, meant something different to the locals who toughed out winter versus those who spent summers only in Antrim County. Both groups felt they belonged in the community, even though they had very different experiences in town. People who came for only one week a year still identified this place as their home away from home. The congregation was inundated with cottage-goers and transient folks who were on their way back home from vacation or were just starting their week or two away by the lake in the tip of the mitten in Michigan— yet the congregation made intentional efforts to help each person feel they belonged to the church on the Sunday they were there. And those who called Bellaire home year-round crafted a sense of belonging that did not diminish the gifts of those who were passing through: they still worked to call everyone by name. This simple act of naming was holy.

The church proudly called themselves a "multi denominational Presbyterian Church." I admit, the contradictory identity was a struggle to explain without living in that space. They were founded by the Presbyterian Church (USA) as a mission to the community in the 1980s, but they felt called to serve all people, from all Christian backgrounds, while those folks visited the community.

I've never felt so connected to a community in such a short period of time, even though I only stayed for four years. The village did so many things to make my family feel we belonged in Bellaire. When the weekly newspaper ran a story about our family moving to town, they gave as much attention to the origins of our names as they did my educational background. Our children, Denali and Bryce, are named after national parks. The community learned that bit of trivia about our family early and made sure to honor their names by constantly introducing us by name—not just as the new pastor but as Andrew, Rachell, Denali, and Bryce (who was born two years after we arrived). When my wife and I eventually left to take a new call in downstate Michigan, we wept tears of sadness and deep gratitude for this wonderful community where we felt so at home.

The final worship service ended with communion celebrated by intinction. As one of the servers of the sacrament, I saw each person receive the elements and had the pleasure of continuing their great tradition of saying each person's name as they came forward to receive the bread and the cup. *"For you, Violet, Christ's body was broken. For you, Violet, Christ's blood was shed."*

And each person replied that day by saying, *"And also for you, Andrew."*

One of the last people to come forward was a running partner of mine. Jon was the same age as I and was newly engaged to be married. He was the best friend I had in this community, but he did not attend the church. He came for this final worship service and walked forward for communion. As he walked up, I barely eked out the words before he responded with, *"And also for you, Andrew."*

While each person said my name, each time it sounded a little different, yet not less intimate or meaningful. I knew Jon differently from Violet, the widow whose husband I buried a few months earlier. Both folks knew me by my name and in the celebration of community, we were connected to the same God who called each of us to the table and called us to invite one another by name.

Being known by name in that congregation is still one of the most intimate and meaningful moments I've experienced in worship.

The invitation by name to join in the sacrament is made with this hope in mind—that all will feel called and welcomed to the table. In Isa 43:1, we hear the prophet quoting the voice of God reminding us that we are called by name, and we belong to God: "I have called you by name, and you are mine." This theme of belonging by name is continued most obviously in Jesus's parable of the Good Shepherd in John 10 as the gatekeeper calls the sheep that belong to him by name, and they follow because they know they know to whom they belong. To be known by a vocational title or role is not the same as being known by our name, by our sense of self-identification. To be called and claimed by name is a powerful experience of ownership by God and the safety and security found therein. We are known within the community when we share this identity with others. Sharing who we are and how we want to be known is a powerful way of experiencing God's call in our lives. When we share our preferred pronouns and names with others we do so with a vulnerability and honesty that demonstrates who we are, how we wish to be known, and how we might truly belong to one another in the Body of Christ. We make ourselves available to be understood.

Years after leaving the church in Bellaire I made a slight vocational shift and accepted a call as the college chaplain for my alma mater. Though I had graduated from Alma College seventeen years earlier, I was not returning home to a place where I was already known. I was new to this community and my point of reference to the campus was rooted in experiences from a generation prior to my arrival. To further complicate things, I joined Alma College as their chaplain mid-year, beginning my ministry midway through the second semester. Because of the timing, the students had already spent most of their year together. It was an unusual time to have a new staff person begin.

Though the chaplain search process and hiring procedure allowed me the opportunity to meet a small number of students prior to my arrival, it was quite different from my introductions to congregations as their new pastor. I entered a campus that had engaged in significant intentional work on community building during orientation at the start of the fall semester. Since that time, sports teams had practiced, competed, and bonded together. Arts ensembles had performed and adjusted to new voices and skill sets, becoming choirs and bands with individuals made to feel a part of their groups. Clubs, Greek organizations, and affinity groups were in full swing by the time I began my ministry. Previous work by the administration at the Alma was both intentional and experiential. Helping a student feel they belonged was a key strategy for addressing declining retention and persistence percentages.

The college chaplain was expected to be with students and help them feel connected as part of this belonging initiative. My directive was to know the students and be known by them—yet I was an unknown person who entered as an outsider. I was a transplant into their existing campus community and I joined at the midpoint of the academic year's community narrative.

I had expectations, experiences, and memories about my alma mater that were formed in a reality from twenty years earlier. I remembered worshiping in the same chapel, yet my memories revolved around people who were no longer there and experiences that were personal to my experience but not communal. I was not known as Andrew, but as "the new chaplain."

Weekly chapel services were expected to be led by the chaplain. During these Sunday evening gatherings, the community celebrated an ecumenical, multi-denominational form of communion. While roots of my Reformed heritage were obvious in their approach, it was still a new liturgy to me that felt unique to the college chapel community. Their recent tradition called for the officiant to serve the elements to each person individually. Memories of my first call in Bellaire came flooding back. Students who came forward for communion were encouraged to say their name so I would know them, and they would get to know me as the new chaplain. It also provided me with the name to say back to them as communion was served.

Allie, for you, Christ's body was broken.
Gene, for you, Christ's blood was shed.

I worried it might feel a bit forced, but the students adopted this new practice of saying their name to the chaplain before the chaplain repeated it back in the context of the liturgy. The difference between this naming experience and the one I enjoyed in Bellaire was the great variety I found in the names they provided. They used their preferred names, their full names, partial names, and nicknames. From week to week, they might use a different name but each identity felt sincere and meaningful in that moment. While I may be rooted in Andrew as my name, I know there are others who feel an affinity to a variety of names. Some students were trying on new versions of their names now that they were on their own at college. Jenny became Jennifer and Chris became Christopher. It felt different than providing your preferred name for the college database.

It was the name that they wished to be known by in that moment and it was rooted in a ritualized religious experience that allowed space for connection to one another through God.

Those names we spoke together had meaning, whether they had been given to the students or they were chosen for themselves. There is something powerful about others understanding that meaning and repeating that name back to you with an intimacy that comes from being known.

God's knowledge of us by name invites this belonging that we are called to share with one another through our desire to know each other as we wish to be known. We are known by the name that God calls each of us as one of God's own sheep in the flock, and then we speak these names back to each other.

Chapter 13

Becoming the Body

Belonging in Paul's Letters and Today

ZEN HESS

Introduction

IN ANCIENT AND CONTEMPORARY times, individual and collective life is marked by gathering. The Greco-Roman world, like today, brimmed with opportunities for participating in communal life, in various ways and for various reasons. One especially popular form of socializing in the Greco-Roman world was joining "associations." Associations were typically small groups—usually twenty to thirty people—that formed around a shared aspect of their members' lives, like a shared occupation, ethnicity, religion, neighborhood, or household. Associations flourished in villages and cities all around the ancient Mediterranean world. By some estimates, in the second century CE, one in three free men in urban areas belonged to an association. It is no surprise, then, that we have found thousands of inscriptions and papyri from associations, giving us detailed glimpses into these groups' common lives, from their group bylaws to receipts for the wine they shared at their monthly meetings.

I find associations fascinating. In my work as a New Testament scholar, pastor, and member of a local community, I find associations essential to a common life. These groups, as John Kloppenborg puts it, were contexts for "connecting and belonging in the ancient city."[1] And so, each associational inscription and papyri provides a glimpse of the way at least some ancient people formed, sustained, and enhanced sites of belonging. No two associations were identical. Yet, we have so many records from associations that we can begin to identify common practices ancient associations used to facilitate belonging in the Greco-Roman world.

What is more, for Christians today, associations give us context and perspective for thinking with the New Testament and early Christian writings about practices of belonging among the earliest Christian groups. By comparing associations and what we find in the New Testament, we see many similarities between Christian groups and associations. At the same time, we will notice differences. And this is where things get interesting. The differences in practices of belonging commonly used by associations and those described in the New Testament hint at how Christ's life, death, and resurrection or the coming of the Spirit gave rise to distinct ideas and practices of belonging in the first century of the church's life.

In this meditation, I think with Paul specifically about belonging. What is belonging in the wake of Christ's death and resurrection or in the light of the Spirit's coming? And what practices did Paul believe would cultivate and sustain belonging in fledgling, sometimes deeply-divided, Christian groups? Is it possible to read Paul's letters as epistles on belonging? In what follows, I read Paul's letters in conversation with the inscriptions and papyri of ancient associations, noting along the way similarities and differences that enable us to recognize key practices of belonging. Paul emphasized practices that unite the body, like the Lord's Supper and sharing the gifts of the Spirit, and Paul urged Christian groups to discern their body so that all may flourish. As it turns out, "fledgling, sometimes deeply divided Christian groups" is a decent descriptor of many churches in the West today. So, along the way, I will attempt to build the bridge between the ancient Mediterranean world and our own, hoping that this meditation will help us in our practicing and reimagining belonging.

Uniting the Body

Gathering mattered for ancient associations. Most groups came together at least monthly, sometimes gathering for additional meals to celebrate a festival, to memorialize a recently deceased member, or some other occasion.

1. Kloppenborg, *Christ's Associations*.

Monthly meetings often included a communal meal, usually a simple meal of wine and bread. Their gatherings were meant to be jovial affairs. One group even banned discussing group business at their banquet to keep the conversation peaceful! Beyond the meal, meeting agendas differed from one group to the next. For example, at the meeting of a group devoted to a certain deity, cultic or ritual components would have played a more prominent role than in the meeting of a group founded by the local salt merchants (although every ancient association had some connection to a deity, no matter how little that may have been reflected in their actual meetings). Gathering was the cornerstone practice by which they facilitated belonging.

Association meetings facilitated belonging in many ways. Most simply, sharing a meal gave members an opportunity to deepen interpersonal relationships. In addition to monthly meetings, some groups required members to gather to drink beer with a man whose son died, comforting a fellow member in their grief. Beyond the simple act of being together, groups typically structured and scripted their meals, purposefully ordering and ritualizing their gathering. This invited members to participate and contribute in ways that deepened their sense of belonging, ensuring members that they were not passive recipients but active participants in the construction and enactment of group life. Likewise, many groups required most or all members to contribute monthly to cover the costs of their meeting, while others used a model where each leader provided the meal in turn. Each of these contribution models required members to "buy in," as it were. Providing money to supply wreaths for the crowning ceremony or wood for the fire served to confirm that their members were integral to the group.

Early Christian groups also met regularly. In fact, like other Jewish groups, Christian groups gathered *more* frequently, at least once a week (Acts 20:7; 1 Cor 16:2; Rev 1:10). This means that Christian groups had forty more gatherings per year than associations who met only once a month. Christian groups also ate together. Undoubtedly, like members of associations, members of Christian groups had to contribute financially in some way to cover the costs of so many more meetings each year. So, on the one hand, Christian groups looked a lot like other associations in that they gathered regularly and ate together, facilitating belonging in similar ways. On the other hand, their meetings happened far more often. This provided Christian groups more opportunities to connect and deepen relationships between members.

Perhaps more significantly, Christian groups differed in that they understood their gatherings as a means of incorporation into a transformative eschatological reality. That is, while some in religious associations believed their deity invited them to their group's dinner or was present with them during it, they did not typically consider their monthly meetings to be the event in which members jointly participated in and became the body of their deity. This is, however, what Paul thought. Describing the Lord's Supper, Paul writes to the Corinthians, saying, "The cup of blessing that we bless, is it not a sharing in the blood of Christ? The bread that we break, is it not a sharing in the body of Christ? Because there is one bread, we who are many are one body, for we all partake of the one bread" (1 Cor 10:16–17). Moreover, Paul expects the Corinthians to set apart time in their gatherings for members to utilize their spiritual gifts. These gifts were given specifically for the building up of Christ's body in ways that would bless members and confirm to outsiders that God is present with the Christian group (1 Cor 12–14). Such mutual spiritual edification was not a usual component of associational gatherings. Paul's emphasis on sharing individual spiritual gifts for communal edification underscores the kind of belonging Paul thought Christ group gatherings would produce through their distinct acts of worship and devotion. Taken together, the Lord's Supper and sharing the gifts of the Spirit transformed the individual members into one body of belonging. This was a belonging that intertwined social and spiritual relationships, a belonging that went far beyond the room, connecting members of Christian groups to other Christ devotees in far off countries and, consequently, to the risen Lord.

So, in some ways, early Christian groups looked like many other associations: gathering regularly, eating meals together, and curating spaces that promoted a sense of belonging. Likewise, in their gatherings, churches today often use practices of belonging borrowed from other social institutions. Such borrowing is in line with the spirit of Paul's letters. After all, Paul is the one who became like a Greek to the Greeks and like a Jew to the Jews (1 Cor 9:20)! Even so, Paul would urge us not to lose sight of the core practices of belonging that were instituted by Christ (i.e., the Lord's Supper, 1 Cor 11:23) and by the Spirit (i.e., sharing spiritual "fruits" and "gifts"). These practices were instituted to facilitate a belonging that conforms to the gospel. As we seek to practice and reimagine belonging today, how might we hold the tension between adopting familiar, cultural practices of belonging and maintaining—perhaps emphasizing anew—those practices which create distinctly Christ-shaped, Spirit-filled belonging?

Discerning the Body

The Spirit-filled work of discerning the shape of belonging was carried out in the company of others, through associations. In general, associations were open and accessible to a wide variety of people. Memberships could include women and men, enslaved and free, people of various ethnicities. Of course, the kind of group sometimes entailed a level of exclusivism, like occupational or certain religious associations. For example, you couldn't *usually* be in the local stonemason guild if you were not a stonemason. But, in general, associations did not put many limits on who could join.

Scholars have suggested, however, at least one way in which associations excluded one particular social category of people: the poor. There were always costs associated with group life. Groups had to pay to rent or build a meeting place, to buy food and wine for meetings, to purchase crowns and monuments for honorifics, to bury deceased members, and so on. Usually, groups covered the costs of their communal life by collecting membership contributions, which each member was required to pay monthly. These contributions were often manageable enough for members earning a middling economic wage, a point easily deduced from the widespread popularity of associations throughout the Greco-Roman world. Yet, for those living at or below subsistence level, the monthly cost of membership would have been prohibitive. This is not to say that people in financial straits didn't organize their own groups, which simply didn't have the resources to leave much of a trace in the historical record, but it does mean that associations did not generally worry about accommodating those who couldn't pay in. This is seen in a note scribbled on the back of a papyrus receipt: "Since I am in poor condition and unable to make contributions to the association, I ask that you accept my resignation. Farewell."[2]

This does not mean that associations never supported members experiencing financial hardship. Several groups included in their bylaws requirements about how either the group as a whole or individual members were to come alongside members experiencing some kind of financial difficulty. One group committed to advocating for and supplying food to members imprisoned for debts. Another group financially penalized

---

2. Ascough et al., *Associations in the Greco-Roman World*, 173.

members who failed to give money to another member who asked for help (unless the member swore an oath that they couldn't afford to help). Many associations practiced forms of mutual care and provision, at least for members who were experiencing a temporarily hard time. Even so, they neither made themselves accessible for those living below the subsistence level, nor did they extend their financial care to those beyond the boundaries of their associational membership.

Paul thought it was the calling of Christian groups to welcome the poor. Paul eagerly agreed to "remember the poor," the singular imperative given to him by the Jerusalem leaders after they affirmed his ministry among the gentiles (Gal 2:10). Remembering the poor is not a novel idea within ancient Judaism. We find calls to care for the poor throughout the Jewish Scriptures, not just in the Prophets but also in the Law and the Writings as well as in the Dead Sea Scrolls and rabbinic literature. So, like other ancient Jews, Paul was zealous to remember the poor in his ministry. Indeed, when including the poor during the Lord's Supper sparked a conflict in Corinth, Paul addressed the issue in the strongest possible terms: "Now in the following instructions I do not commend you, because when you come together it is not for the better but for the worse" (1 Cor 11:17).

Importantly, in his correction to the Corinthians, Paul offered a guiding practice, which I think is key for reflecting on our practices of belonging today. After describing the issue—that some Corinthians are shaming others by indulging in an excessive meal while "those who have nothing" leave the Lord's Supper hungry—Paul urges the Corinthians to "discern the body" (1 Cor 11:29). Discerning the body is not, or at least not *only*, an act of internal self-reflection. In my opinion, the most compelling interpretation of "discerning the body" is that Paul expects all the Corinthians to be attentive to the needs and the dignity of fellow members. Discerning the body is ensuring even the supposedly weaker, less honorable, less respectable members of Christ's body are welcomed and shown hospitality at the Lord's Supper (1 Cor 12:22). The Corinthians are invited to give themselves to one another, to guard one another, to truly share with one another. After all, they are one body and one in the Lord (1 Cor 10:17; see also Rom 12:5; 1 Cor 12:27). Discerning the body was an ongoing practice and negotiation of belonging.

So it is for Christian institutions today. Like in Corinth, Christian groups in America today are reckoning with questions of inclusion in a variety of ways. Reflecting on the experience of disabled people in the church, Erin Raffety has suggested that we need to move from models of inclusion to models of justice.[3] This involves shifting the way we frame ministry from "ministry for" to "ministry with." For example, ministry *for* disabled people keeps people with disabilities at an arm's length, welcoming them in the door, perhaps, but not making space for them at the table. Ministry *with* disabled people reframes the whole community as one body with various gifted parts who all minister alongside one another for the sake of the gospel. The shift from ministry "for" to "with" needs to take place at many other junctures in the Church's congregational life too. How do we do ministry *with* those experiencing racism? Sexism? Incarceration? Addiction?

Or, circling back to Paul and the Corinthians, how might we do ministry *with* those experiencing poverty? I think this is what Paul was trying to get the Corinthians to do when he called on them to discern the body. He wanted the wealthier Corinthians to realize that their call to include "those who have nothing" was not just to let them in the door, as if proximity equaled belonging. Paul called the wealthy Corinthians to share not just resources with those in need, but their very lives (1 Thess 2:8). They were to become the body of Christ together, those who have and those who have not.

As churches and institutions today practice and reimagine belonging, we ought to discern our own bodies (i.e., congregations, institutions), asking whose experiences we have failed or refused to consider, who we have shamed or humiliated by the very practices that are meant to draw us into deeper communion with one another and with Christ, and how these practices of belonging stand in continuity and discontinuity with Christians throughout time. For example, a congregation in Black Mountain, North Carolina, has inscribed "Has everyone been fed?" on the front of their communion table, a fitting visual reminder of Paul's call to discern the body.

Conclusion

At the heart of Paul's gospel is his belief that Christ's death and resurrection unite those who have long been divided by the power of sin. "There is," Paul writes, "no longer Jew or Greek, there is no longer slave or free, there is no longer male and female; for all of you are one in Christ Jesus" (Gal 3:28). We might rephrase the end of this verse ever so slightly: "You

---

3. Raffety, *From Inclusion to Justice*, 1–61.

all belong to one another in Christ Jesus." Paul puts this belief to work when he writes to Christian groups in Galatia, Corinth, and elsewhere, inviting them to attend to the fractures in their communal bodies. Paul's belief in Christ's overcoming of division leads him to encourage Christian groups to adopt practices of belonging. These practices did not differ in every way from other associations but differed in subtle yet significant ways. The differences derive from Paul's Christ-shaped understanding of belonging. He urged Christian groups to gather more regularly, to understand their gatherings as experiences of transformation, and to welcome the culturally despised as full, respected members. In these ways, Christian groups would become more than just jovial get-togethers; they would become sites of transformative belonging, where individuals were changed and bound together by the Spirit of Christ.

As Christian churches and institutions practice and reimagine belonging today, Paul invites us to cling to long-standing Christian practices: sharing meals, blessing one another with our spiritual gifts, and welcoming the ones society has excluded. At the same time, Paul urges us to remember that through these practices the Spirit facilitates a belonging beyond simple "inclusion" and beyond the various polarizations we carry with us into relationships. We become Christ's body, bound to one another and to Christ.

Bibliography

Ascough, Richard S., et al., eds. *Associations in the Greco-Roman World: A Source Book*. Waco, TX: Baylor University Press, 2012.

Kloppenborg, John S. *Christ's Associations: Connecting and Belonging in the Ancient City*. New Haven, CT: Yale University Press, 2019.

Raffety, Erin. *From Inclusion to Justice: Disability, Ministry, and Congregational Leadership*. Studies in Religion, Theology, and Disability. Waco, TX: Baylor University Press, 2022.

PART 5
Barriers and Rupture

Chapter 14

Beyond Assimilation, Toward a Story of "You Belong Here"

Chris Dela Cruz

"GO AWAY FROM ME!"

I was a middle schooler, too old to be disrespecting my Lola like that. But there I was, pouting in our kitchen, yelling at Lola—the Tagalog word for grandmother—to leave. I don't remember the specifics that inspired this, almost definitely something trivial. But even accounting for hormones running through my adolescent body, there was something deeper motivating me to channel fury at her, something like rage, something like grief, but harsher, cutting deeper. Something like self-hate.

Lola was visiting our family in the majority white suburbs of New Jersey. And, like any middle schooler, I spent those years wanting to belong. I didn't want to be different. At a young age, I hid the smell and sight of my packed lunch Sisig leftovers at the hint of kids making faces. As I moved on to middle school, being a short brown kid made me an easy target for all sorts of actions that we would now name as bullying—receiving daily verbal put downs and punches to my arm just for the hell of it, enduring a rotation of various sexually explicit disparaging nicknames, assuming as normal constantly being made fun of, me waiting for the bus being the kid in the center as a circle of boys tossing my backpack over my head so I couldn't reach.

PART 5: BARRIERS AND RUPTURE

Without any larger systemic analysis of race relations in America, I already intuited as a child there was this hierarchical ranking of "white" and "non-white." My internalized response to this intuition was that the best way out of otherness was to move closer to whiteness. If I performed enough acceptability to whiteness, then I would belong, I told myself. Asian Americans whose accents were too thick and food tastes too smelly were labeled Fresh Off the Boat or FOBs—a label we gleefully placed on our own Asian peers. I laughed with other Asian friends as we proudly called ourselves coconuts—brown on the outside, white on the inside.

This was my self-imposed calling. To belong through filtering out my difference. But Lola represented everything that would set me apart as an Other. Her accented exchange of the "P" sound for "F," her lack of knowledge of basic American cultural milestones, her mere presence an embarrassment to friends who came over and to see that I was not fully like them.

Lola embodied all the ways I did not belong.

"*Why aren't you listening to me? Go away!!*"

Lola stood there, frozen and shaken at the sight of her little *apo* she once held in her arms, now crying for her to leave. After a moment, she did just that.

Lola, of course, did not deserve to be designated the innocent vessel for my unprocessed self-hate. I still carry guilt for the ways I hurt her and carried resentment toward my family, and I ultimately take responsibility for my actions.

At the same time, I was a kid. And as I got older, I slowly realized I was not the only Asian American in my generation who carried this self-hate. In just one testimony out of many, Kelly Marie Tran, after a slew of online harassment for the "crime" of being a woman of color in a Star Wars movie, wrote in an editorial of the shame growing up "for the things that made me different, a shame for the culture from which I came."[1] As an adult, I read, heard, and personally listened to stories from Asian Americans, first or second generation, growing up in the 1980s, 1990s, and early 2000s. They described experiences of invisibility and self-doubt, of having to live up to Model Minority stereotypes, of having to mold their stories onto the white people stories that dominated our culture, of dwelling in liminal spaces, of wanting to be seen as white, and of self-hate against their own culture and family.

---

1. Tran, "I Won't Be Marginalized by Online Harassment," 12.

Belonging as Assimilation

I now have some language and framework to describe this collective experience—the pressure of assimilation imposed on Asian Americans as the ticket to belonging in white dominant United States.

Growing up, the United States prided itself as a "melting pot" of sorts. Look at all the diverse colors coming together! The problem, of course, is that this particular process of melting imposed a blending of sorts that ends up being white washing. Everyone belongs, as long as everyone adheres to whiteness. It is a system of belonging through dominance, with the rules set by the dominant privileged, enforced through practices of violence and erasure.

This "ticket to belonging" has its foundation particularly in anti-Blackness and indigenous erasure. By definition, a "model minority" implies minorities who are not models. The "model minority" myth was created by white America self-selecting certain Asian immigrants as Cold War-era propaganda to squash calls for equality for Black Americans—these minorities can do it, why can't you?

And what even is this belonging? To use a Pauline framework, it is false salvation by works and merit, demanding constant performance and self-harm through denying of self.

I grieve what I have lost in the pursuit of belonging through white assimilation. I recall one pivotal moment for me: when I was four years old, my white preschool teacher told my immigrant mother that she needed to stop teaching Tagalog at home, because I was behind in speaking English. Never mind all we know now about the developmental benefits of learning multiple languages as a child. Who was this teacher to tell a family that their native tongue couldn't flourish in their own home? But my mother wanted the best for her children, and so she stopped intentionally teaching me Tagalog. Language is fundamentally tied to connection with family and understanding of culture. For me, this meant a whole childhood having this disconnection from my roots, with not understanding the heart language of my own mother and father, the language they feel and process and dream in.

In the process of pursuing white assimilation for belonging, we lose ourselves. Our connection to our ancestors, the ties that bind genuine community, the languages that ground us, the empowerment and resilience that comes from collective pride. We lose a sense of identity that comes from the realness of place, and instead we find a hollowed core tied to the hierarchy of race.

And for what? Finally, a spot at the chosen few? The chosen few don't seem to have peace in their own whiteness. Racialized backlash has become common, and belonging through whiteness is so fragile that it takes book bans, AP curriculum erasure, and encroaching police states and resentment politics just to maintain it. Assimilation, in the lived-out practices of white supremacy, simply does not nurture belonging.

As a pastor, I am entrusted with, among many other things, passing down the stories, values, and theologies of our Christian faith tradition. I struggle regularly with a vocation that places me in the white institution that used a robust theology of assimilation to violently colonize the land of my ancestors. This was true for both Catholics through Spanish conquest and Protestants through American conquest. President William McKinley literally called its policy toward the Philippines "benevolent assimilation," an incredibly paternalistic attitude of civilizing the "savages" and "substituting the mild sway of justice and right for arbitrary rule." Never mind that Filipinos asserted their own will and right to rule over themselves after the Spanish American War. And that the United States was willfully and violently ignoring Filipino agency, resulting in the Philippine–American War that cost, by some estimates, over a million Filipino lives.

Most insultingly, President McKinley told his advisors he was inspired to pursue this doctrine "benevolent assimilation" precisely after praying to God, since "there was nothing left for us to do but to take them all, and to educate the Filipinos, and uplift and civilize and Christianize them, and by God's grace do the very best we could by them, as our fellowmen for whom Christ also died. . . . And then I went to bed, and went to sleep, and slept soundly."[2]

Belonging and Pastoral Ministry

I struggle with my calling as Presbyterian pastor all the time. How can I justify to my ancestors being a part of an institution that perpetuated this? How can I pass down a theological tradition that laid the foundation for this without interrogating it? Is my place in the white, mainline church the culmination of my assimilation journey, pouring out my energy and resources and time and energy and my heart and literal soul to this white

2. Rusling, "Interview with President William McKinley."

institution that it often feels just wants me for its diversity quota? I don't have easy answers for myself. But I do wonder.

I wonder if our Christian tradition and origin stories do, in fact, have at their roots a theology of belonging beyond assimilation. After all, despite Christian theology justifying empire and colonizations and white supremacy and patriarchy and conquest and LGBTQ persecution and economic inequality, liberation movements throughout history have also drawn from these same wells for inspiration.

I wonder if the Christian narrative could be told or retold for the twenty-first century, as a story of the pursuit of belonging beyond assimilation. That when God declared, "let there be light" and "let there be night" and "let the waters bring forth swarms of living creatures" and "let us make humankind in our image" and declared all creation "good," God was also declaring at each point, "You Belong Here." That this word of "You Belong Here" echoes through the journey of the people of God, through the stars that Sarah and Abraham fixed their gaze on marking their descendants, through the roar of the parted Red Sea and the celebratory singing of Miriam for those newly freed from the chains of slavery, through the still, small voice of the prophet Elijah who wanted to end his life, through the pouting Jonah who couldn't sense the expanding grace of God beyond the belly of a big fish, through the declaration of Mary and Miriam of resurrection in their midst, through the shock of Peter and Paul by the God of their ancestors expanding table fellowship beyond traditional boundaries.

And ultimately, that this word of "You Belong Here" is found incarnate, embodied, in our Christian tradition's central Word, Jesus Christ. Jesus, who was rejected by the center of religion and the state and spent his life in the margins with the poor and oppressed and outcast. Jesus, whose crucifixion on the cross was the world's apocalyptic declaration of not belonging through murder and therefore literal erasure. You, the poor and oppressed, you who are not enough, you who are defined by the mistakes and sins we put on you, you who threaten the status quo of empire, you who refuse to assimilate to the ways of the world: You. Do. Not. Belong. Here.

And Jesus, whose resurrection proclaims, in embodied glory, "Yes, I do belong here. And therefore you belong here. You all belong here."

I wonder if this is how we could tell our story as travelers within the Christian tradition. What would it mean? What would it mean for practicing a different way toward true belonging, away from assimilation? What if belonging started not by defining a center to assimilate toward but by standing in the margins like Jesus?

It feels deeper than simply "celebrating difference." It would mean cultivating spaces where people could truly grow more authentically into themselves, to be themselves more fully, to flourish in their pursuits of calling and purpose and community and relationship. It would mean not severing roots or identity through place in the pursuit of the false hope of a "melting pot," but people deepening their roots and sense of where they come from.

Cultivating these spaces would necessarily mean tension and struggle. Assimilation is meant to produce homogeneity, and there is a false but understandable longing for peace and tranquility that comes from everyone having a narrow set of values and touchpoints. But if each one of us truly belongs here, then we would have to develop practices to be able to tolerate discomfort and conflict, to be able to communicate and live with one another. It would mean a theology of discipleship that would be more than an intellectual adherence to doctrines, more even than the pursuit of emotional highs that come and go. Instead, it would mean an embodied, daily embrace of letting go into the wind of the Spirit, breathing in the life that comes from sacred communion, breathing out all the habits and learnings of a lifetime of assimilating into a culture of violence and domination.

It would mean wrestling with the gray areas of the distinctions between overall belonging in terms of humanity and creation, versus belonging in smaller spaces defined by the boundaries of mission or interests or shared experience or culture. Whether a religious community, or an organizing space, or a cultural club, or a group of friends or family, or a nation, we would need to be intentional in interrogating carefully which boundaries and practices are being used for further rootedness, and which ones are used for erasure and assimilation.

It wouldn't be easy. But it would be the only real way toward a belonging that moves beyond the logic of assimilation.

Belief and Belonging Beyond Assimilation

In the later years of undergraduate college, after years of atheism, I found myself back as a practitioner of Christian faith, part of a Christian community. I remember, after some time of processing embarrassment and shame,

I came to my parents and told them, holding my newly purchased Study Bible in hand, that I was a Christian again.

I remember my mother responding, "I'm happy for you. And I never doubted your journey. Because your Lola has been praying for you for years, every day." The same Lola toward whom I harbored all this rage and resentment, the same Lola who I yelled at to go away all those years ago. She saw me as her *apo*, and she prayed that I would feel belonging through relationship with the God she found belonging in.

In that way, she knew the eternal truth inside her bones that it would take me decades to learn for myself. I belong here. And so do you.

Bibliography

Rusling, James. "Interview with President William McKinley." In *The Life of William McKinley*, 2:109–11. New York: Houghton Mifflin, 1916.

Tran, Kelly Marie. "I Won't Be Marginalized by Online Harassment." *New York Times*, August 21, 2018. https://www.nytimes.com/2018/08/21/movies/kelly-marie-tran.html?

Chapter 15

Transformative Belonging in Higher Education

Kevin J. Villegas

So many sights, sounds, people, and experiences inspire me in my work toward cultivating a sense of belonging for students in higher education. College students—like all human beings—have a longing to belong. The desire to feel like we are a part of something beyond ourselves is an innate quality we all share—whether we are conscious of it or not. To belong is to be grounded. It is to know with absolute assurance that you are in a safe, nurturing, and trustworthy space. In light of this, altruistic educators and administrators at colleges and universities in the United States are more and more realizing the importance of tending to a sense of belonging for members of their communities. It is vital to the success and wellbeing of students, faculty, and staff.[1] Indeed, the work of cultivating trustworthy environments in spaces of higher learning is an educational imperative that has the potential to promote transformative belonging, rooting us all in the beauty and goodness of our shared humanity.

To be sure, there is some irony to be found here. Throughout much of higher education's history in the US, certain groups of people were intentionally excluded.[2] With few exceptions, most institutions implicitly and

---

1. McCaig, "Factors That Lead to Greater College Success."
2. Thelin, *History of American Higher Education*, 107.

explicitly conveyed messages to Catholics, Jews, women, people of color, and individuals with certain disabilities that they did not belong there. Men in power largely agreed—in principle and practice—who belonged at their colleges and universities and who did not belong. Access to a college or university education seemed to only belong to the advantaged of society. As one historian noted, there were policies "of vigorous affirmative action for the privileged" in place.[3]

The most obvious barriers to gaining access to higher education for those historically excluded have largely been addressed as society has progressed toward being more inclusive. Nevertheless, cultural artifacts and customs from centuries of exclusionary practices linger like a fine mist at most institutions, continuing to convey—albeit subtle—messages that certain individuals and groups of people belong more than others. As an example, it was not until the Americans with Disabilities Act (ADA) was signed into law in 1990, that individuals with certain disabilities broadly even had the physical means to attend most colleges and universities due to campus infrastructure and building design limitations. Yet decades after the passage of the ADA, students with disabilities continue to face barriers to belonging. Frustrating experiences like navigating narrow spaces, having no ramps to buildings, and infrequent curb cuts on sidewalks send messages to people with mobility issues that they are not seen. Well-intentioned signs like "Bears Take the Stairs" (posted on the elevator of an administration building on my campus, meant to encourage physical fitness) can leave students, faculty, staff, and alumni in wheelchairs feeling like they're not Baylor Bears (as they cannot take the stairs). Thankfully, the sign has since been removed.

Names of schools, campus buildings, statues, plaques, historic photos and art, and the largely homogenous composition of college and university boards, senior administration, and whole departments that primarily come from the historically dominant social group can have similar effects on one's sense of belonging—particularly on individuals from groups who have been historically excluded and marginalized. It is not too difficult to notice present-day barriers that can negatively impact one's sense of belonging in practice. But where barriers exist, so also exist opportunities.

Attention in higher education to students' sense of belonging has increased dramatically in the past several years as student success and retention efforts have been given more attention. In one study designed

3. Karabel, *Chosen*, 199.

PART 5: BARRIERS AND RUPTURE

to identify characteristics that contribute to success of college students, *sense of belonging* is a primary contributor.[4] There are sense-of-belonging taskforces and committees and working groups at colleges and universities. Schools regularly measure their students' sense of belonging, using it as a metric to determine the likelihood of retention or attrition. We have even seen an increasing number of newly created or retitled positions that have the word *belonging* in them. Clearly one's sense of belonging matters a great deal in learning environments.

In the context of higher education, scholar Terrell Strayhorn defines *sense of belonging* as an individual's "perceived social support on campus, a feeling of connectedness, or that one is important to others," whether this is real or perceived.[5]

While this is a helpful definition, notice the words *perceived* and *feeling*, and the phrase *to others*. It is ultimately about an individual's *sense* of things. Do individual students *perceive* that there is a network of social support for them at school? Do they *feel* a connection to the school and to others? Do they have the impression that they matter to those around them? Our feelings can be informed and validated by experience, but what we feel or sense does not always equate to reality. Our senses can deceive or misinform us, and our feelings can lie to us.

When my son Benjamin was four years old, we lived in an older home that had a basement. Like most young children, Benjamin was afraid to go down to the basement alone. If someone was with him, he felt safe and was fine to be downstairs. On one occasion, Benjamin and I were down in the basement playing. He had his back turned toward me occupied with some toy and I took a moment to check something out in another part of the basement that was around a corner and out of his line of sight. Suddenly, I heard Benjamin scream "Dad?!?," next noticing him dart past me to run up the stairs. "Benjamin," I said. "I'm right here." He turned back and ran toward me, arms in the air, to be picked up and held. "It's alright. I wouldn't leave you down here alone," I told him reassuringly.

Benjamin sensed that I was not with him, that I was gone. In actuality, I was there with him the whole time. True, he did not sense me through his eyesight, but I was still there. Even as we age and mature, what we sense isn't always accurate. Nevertheless, experience shapes perception and perception shapes our grasp of reality. No doubt colleges and universities who

---

4. Han et al., "Effects of Academic Mindsets."
5. Strayhorn, *College Students' Sense of Belonging*, 16.

invite people (students/faculty/staff) to join their respective communities believe that the people belong there. Yet how individuals experience the spaces at their school matters. Just saying someone belongs somewhere is not enough. It must be demonstrated. For incoming and established students, faculty, and staff, it is still important to engage in effective practices that tend to the sense of belonging of each community member. However, we must also begin to promote transformative belonging—a *deep knowing* that we truly do belong. It is moving beyond a need to *sense* that we belong to, instead, a deep knowing that we inherently and utterly belong, forever and always, to one another and to God in Christ (Col 3:3).

On average, nearly three-quarters of a million students begin attending four-year, residential colleges and universities each year in pursuit of undergraduate degrees. The number is smaller for those selecting to attend private, faith-based institutions—but still significant. It is in these faith-based schools that opportunities to promote transformative belonging present themselves more readily and acutely. This is not to imply that the idea of belonging is not important to educators and administrators at non-faith-based institutions. It is only because—as a Christian who has worked in faith-based higher education for nearly twenty years—I view the concept of transformative belonging as something much more profound than merely addressing external factors that contribute to a sense of belonging for students, faculty, and staff. Indeed, it is even becoming increasingly difficult for state-funded institutions to perform work that affects belonging given recently passed legislation hampering efforts toward addressing matters of diversity, equity, and inclusion. Moreover, faith-based colleges and universities can offer students a *telos*—a clear aim that reflects their shared values—for their communities of learning in ways that secular institutions simply cannot. For my work and institutional service, intentional and healthy expressions of faith play an essential role in forming identity and promoting transformative belonging.

The Hope of Transformative Belonging

I write these ideas as a believing follower of the life and teachings of Jesus of Nazareth. This core identity of mine animates me and is where I personally encounter transformative belonging for myself. It also informs the collaborative, holistic student development work that I do toward creating trustworthy spaces where transformative belonging can be shared, experienced, and internalized.

Paul, in his epistle to the churches in Rome, told his fellow Christians to not be conformed to the patterns of this world, but to be transformed by the renewing of their minds (Rom 12:2). Our move toward belonging does not involve having to look and act like any other group, being formed with the prevailing cultural or societal patterns (i.e., conformed). And it is also beyond seeking to be formed against those patterns (i.e., counter formed). To be *transformed* is to change in character and condition, moving from one state of being to an entirely new one. Quite literally, it is a metamorphosis. And it starts with our minds and in how we think about ourselves and the world.

In higher education, much of what we do is formational. As a cocurricular educator working in Christian higher education to develop students, what I do is sometimes also counter formational. But considering the epidemic of loneliness and anxiety in society—even among people of faith—this is not enough. I assert that we must recommit to practices found in the rich heritage of the contemplative tradition to renew our minds. This has the greatest potential to lead us to experiencing transformative belonging.

On a personal level, this sort of belongingness is something that I've only recently begun to fully experience and realize myself. And it is transformational. As someone who grew up biracial and bicultural, I never quite felt like I belonged. Add that my parents divorced when I was young—which had me going physically back and forth between two different cultures, neither of which I felt entirely at home in—and my feelings of not belonging were exacerbated. When I turned fourteen, I began attending a prestigious private school in New York City where—compared to my peers—I was not as financially well off, contributing to a sense that I did not belong. Like most adolescents, I sought identity and value and belonging in things like participation in sports, the performing arts, through expression of my musical tastes and moving in and out different circles of friends. Striving to fit in with this group or that group, I became quite skilled at adapting in different social settings and environments. Yet a sense of belongingness remained elusive.

No doubt in search of belonging to something greater, I then enlisted in the United States Marine Corps after a failed first semester of college. This gave me a strong sense of belonging for a time, but over the years I grew disillusioned with the military. As work and life continued, I would later get out of the Marine Corps, go back to college, marry, have children, attend seminary, and pursue a career in higher education. But I still never quite felt like I fully belonged in or to something or someplace.

Then I discovered the writings of Thomas Merton, the poetry of Mary Oliver, and the rich tapestry of contemplative Christian monastics and mystics in people like Teresa of Avila, Saint John of the Cross, Julian of Norwich, Meister Eckhart, and the Desert Fathers. Poems and vignettes and writings from or about people like this led me to see things with new eyes. For the first time, I realized that I have always belonged and that I have never not belonged, and that in Christ I am home. To describe how this unfolded is beyond the scope of this chapter, but the result led to my transformation through the thinking of new thoughts (i.e., renewing of the mind) by way of contemplative practices.

In short, this journey led me to recognize the false labels and identities I either held to or sought after to conform to the patterns of this world in search of belonging. In recognizing and naming these labels and identities, I was able to develop an awareness of them, noticing when they began to assert themselves and then put them in proper perspective in light of my true and everlasting identity in Christ. To be sure, this is mostly an inward journey that involves the ongoing learning and practice of things like silence, solitude, and stillness.

The way this shows up in my work as a student development practitioner and administrator is in how I see myself, and so see all things as belonging. It has fundamentally changed how I see people, students in particular. I work to guide students toward this sort of transformative belonging through meaningful programming and mentoring. It compels me to create trustworthy environments where students, faculty and staff feel secure and free enough to ask deep questions and explore their inner selves with greater confidence.

To be in a trustworthy environment does not mean that we won't ever experience anything negative or unsettling in different spaces or through the acts of others. We will be occasionally troubled. We will feel hurt and excluded at times. But our internalized, and increasingly realized, transformative belongingness will serve as a touchstone for us—a homebase to which we can return to be reminded of who we are actually and eternally.

I leave you with a story from the Desert Fathers to contemplate.

> Abba Lot came to Abba Joseph and said:
>
> "Father, according as I am able, I keep my little rule, and my little fast, my prayer, meditation, and contemplative silence; and, according as I am able, I strive to cleanse my heart of thoughts: now what more should I do?"
>
> The elder rose up in reply and stretched out his hands to heaven, and his fingers became lit like ten lamps of fire.
>
> He said: "Why not become fire?"[6]

Beyond working to cultivate a mere sense of belonging in ourselves and others, why not aim to be truly transformed? A realization of our Oneness in Christ.

The work of leading others to experience transformative belonging is sacred. To cultivate trustworthy environments in higher education—spaces where students, faculty, and staff are safe and nurtured—is to reinforce and promote transformative belonging in practice. Moving by faith toward realizing that the deepest well of our existence and identity is in Christ, is to surrender our desire to belong to this group or that group. It is to encounter—and help others to encounter—our true nature and most hidden self in the One in whom we live and move and have our being (Acts 17:28). It is to be transformed, to be home, to utterly belong.

Bibliography

Han, Cheon-Woo, et al. "Effects of Academic Mindsets on College Students' Achievement and Retention." *Journal of College Student Development* 58 (2017) 1119–34.

Karabel, Jerome. *The Chosen: The Hidden History of Admission and Exclusion at Harvard, Yale, and Princeton*. Round Rock, TX: Houghton Mifflin Harcourt, 2005.

McCaig, Amy. "Factors That Lead to Greater College Success." *Science Daily*, May 30, 2017. www.sciencedaily.com/releases/2017/05/170530115102.htm.

Merton, Thomas. *The Wisdom of the Desert*. New York: New Directions, 1970.

Strayhorn, Terrell L. *College Students' Sense of Belonging: A Key to Educational Success for All Students*. New York: Routledge, 2019.

Thelin, John R. *A History of American Higher Education*. Baltimore: Johns Hopkins University Press, 2011.

---

6. Merton, *Wisdom of the Desert*.

Chapter 16

How the Church Becomes the Heart of the Community

Risking Subversive Belonging Together

Janelle Lindsay Adams

"Subversive belonging," Pastor Jay tells me, "means you reject what culture says you need to be thriving and successful." Taking another sip of quickly cooling coffee, Jay continues, "Subversive belonging looks like being in relationship with people who care about you, who check in on you, who share with you."[1] This meditation tells the story of the church Jay formerly pastored, New Hope Presbyterian Church.

By societal standards, this church was not successful. Indeed, a church that once included fifteen hundred members in its heyday in the 1960s is no more; its former members have been engrafted into another congregation.[2] Yet this is also a story of divine presence and resurrection in a congregation that dared to be in relationship with its neighbors in the last decade of its existence. As New Hope Presbyterian's members aged and its finances dwindled, practices of subversive belonging on its campus proliferated.

---

1. For privacy, the names of individuals and organizations have been changed.

2. In the Presbyterian Church (USA), engrafting refers to the process by which members and assets of a declining congregation can become a part of another "receiving congregation."

This story of divine presence and resurrection played out as New Hope Presbyterian Church gave birth to Lattice Ministries, a thriving community hub where newly arrived refugees and individuals born in the United States are growing opportunities for belonging together. The congregation's experiences make clear that the work of subverting the traditional boundaries of belonging—boundaries that serve to include "us" by excluding "them"—is inherently risky. Ethicist Sharon Welch articulates an ethic of risk that encompasses "a redefinition of responsible action, grounding in community, and strategic risk-taking."[3] New Hope Presbyterian's story shows how such an ethic can embolden faith communities to prioritize love for their neighbors over their desire for institutional longevity. In what follows, I explore how one church's embrace of an ethic of risk made new life possible during its ecclesial end-of-life season.

Making Room

Of the first component of an ethic of risk, "a redefinition of responsible action," Sharon Welch suggests that such "action begins where much middle-class thought stops."[4] While those of us with economic and racial privilege can all too quickly fall into despair in the face of failing systems, structural inequality, and entrenched social issues, an ethic of risk insists on acting anyway—finding a place to begin despite the size of the challenge or the unpredictability of the outcome. For the New Hope Presbyterian Church community, this rethinking of the meaning of responsible action began to take root soon after they called Pastor Jay as their minister in the early 2010s, already during a time of congregational decline. Jay would often invite the congregation to think beyond their church walls and reflect on the question, "How does the church become the heart of the community?" With Jay's help, the congregation became increasingly aware of the magnitude of the tragedy of the global forced migration crisis. Located in an area long favored by refugee service agencies for resettlement, New Hope Presbyterian found itself with new neighbors from Sudan to Myanmar, Ethiopia to Nepal, and Afghanistan to the Democratic Republic of Congo. With time and practice, the church came to define responsible action as responding to the "knocks" of all their neighbors and making room for all who walked through their church doors.

3. Welch, *Feminist Ethic of Risk*, 46.
4. Welch, *Feminist Ethic of Risk*, 67.

The first knock on New Hope Presbyterian Church's doors came from Pastor Joseph, a minister from the Democratic Republic of Congo. Joseph was looking for a space for his growing Pan-African congregation, Mulunda Worshiping Community. The New Hope Presbyterian congregation made room for the Mulunda congregation, working with the presbytery to secure funds to renovate unused chapel space for the community. Adlin, who was an elder on New Hope Presbyterian's session and who came to the United States decades earlier from the Caribbean, recalls of this time of change, "We started really trying to figure out how to worship together. It made me see Christianity and the work we do in the name of Christ very differently." She concludes, "If we're not welcoming and creating a welcoming space, where else would we find that?"[5]

The next knock on the door came from Gladys, the founder of Kuumba, a holistic sewing and leadership initiative for women who came to the United States as refugees. Noting how isolating the United States can be for women who have experienced displacement, Gladys, herself an immigrant from Kenya, wanted to create a space where women could learn a skill, build friendships, and informally share resources for navigating the challenges of everyday life. Jay somewhat hesitantly showed Gladys the large, rundown rooms in the church's gym. Gladys enthusiastically committed to join the growing campus community. Soon after, the New Hope Presbyterian congregation jumped into action to assist Kuumba with transforming the unused space into a place of belonging.

At about the same time, Pastor Thang came knocking. He was the minister of a growing Mara-speaking congregation. Before long, worship was happening on campus at all hours on Sundays: New Hope Presbyterian convened in the morning, Mulunda Worshiping Community gathered in the afternoon, and Mara Church worshiped in the evening. Thang tells me that Jay made space not only for his congregation on campus, but also for him personally in Jay's office. The two ministers would work back-to-back and take breaks to discuss everything from systematic theology to the challenges facing their communities. Thang credits Jay with shaping his theology of ministry and contributing to his growing openness to people from very different religious backgrounds.

---

5. The session is the leadership council of each PC(USA) congregation, comprised both of "ruling elders," selected from members of the church, and "teaching elders," the pastor or pastors.

The knocks on New Hope Presbyterian's doors continued as additional immigrant faith communities and nonprofit partners found a place to call home on campus. While the New Hope Presbyterian community could have simply bemoaned the broken systems and inequality that newly arrived refugees face upon arrival to the United States, they instead chose to start somewhere by insistently making room in their sanctuary, in their offices, and at their tables.

Growing a Ruth Community

While feelings of helplessness pose barriers to the important work of subversive belonging, love can make risk-filled action sustainable. The congregation of New Hope Presbyterian Church leaned into a second element of an ethic of risk, "grounding in community,"[6] as they grew their understanding of community to envelop the partners on their campus. As former New Hope Presbyterian member Kay puts it, "We became a multi-church family." This expanded sense of "we" was cultivated through times of shared worship; Thanksgiving feasts with all the campus faith communities, nonprofits, and recreation groups; and their growing commitment to show up for one another whenever a group on campus had a particular need. As they pooled resources, facilitated donation drives, and volunteered to direct traffic for events, New Hope Presbyterian's members began learning how to be accountable in their relationships with the newcomers on campus.

Two biblical stories shaped the congregation's perspective on what it looked like to build a community of love and solidarity, rather than one of charity, guilt, or obligation. First, Pastor Jay frequently invoked Jesus's teachings about the identity of our neighbors. "It's about how broadly you define your neighbor," Jay would preach. "Who's my neighbor? And how am I going to be in a relationship with them?" His challenging response: "If you walk in my door, that makes you my neighbor."

The second powerful theological story that rooted their growing community came from the book of Ruth. Ruth tells Naomi, "Your people shall be my people, and your God my God" (Ruth 1:16). Adlin remembers how visceral the vision of growing a "Ruth community" came to feel for New Hope Presbyterian members. Just as Ruth and Naomi worked hard to cultivate a relationship of care across differences, so too did the New Hope Presbyterian community desire to do so with their neighbors on

---

6. Welch, *Feminist Ethic of Risk*, 162.

and around their campus. Adlin explains, "We wanted to invite belonging, to invite people to come in. They had a story, and it was something that benefited the community. We found a space for them." Peter, a member of the session and himself an immigrant from the United Kingdom, told me about this vision of a mutually caring community. One important part was Jay and the session's insistence that New Hope Presbyterian would not charge their new partners market-rate rent. As Peter recalled, the priority was on relationship over transaction: "We were interested in them, they were interested in us, and it was relational." These commitments deepened as members of the New Hope Presbyterian community practiced showing up for their neighbors. For example, when members of the local Rohingya community organized a protest about the dire situation in Myanmar, church members stood with them. And when the local Somali American association needed a place to meet after having been denied space at other local venues, the New Hope Presbyterian community was ready to make room and offer hospitality once again.

Risking Letting Go

Finally, the New Hope Presbyterian Church community embraced a third element of subversive belonging, "strategic risk taking." They did this each time they chose to care more about being church to their community than about their institutional longevity. Had they leaned into a desire to preserve the church, they might have charged their campus partners higher rent. These market rates would have resulted in these groups needing to move away from the neighborhood in which their community members had resettled. Indeed, this possibility of charging more at times caused tensions between New Hope Presbyterian and the other local congregations. Jay explains that, while some felt that New Hope Presbyterian ought to have been more fiscally strategic, such a choice was not aligned with the path of subversive belonging New Hope was trying to take. As Jay puts it emphatically, "The White church still operates very much in a paradigm of cost and benefit. But [newcomers] are giving us the opportunity to be church in a way that is closer to what Jesus imagined." By resisting the pull to optimize revenue, Jay and his congregation were seeking to create an interdependent community, where all could give freely of what they had and trust they would receive what they needed in turn.

PART 5: BARRIERS AND RUPTURE

The New Hope Presbyterian community also took strategic risks as they invited denominational and local partners into conversations about sustaining the growing campus community. In time, the congregation realized they needed a second pastor on staff to support the community on campus. They also reckoned with the reality that they could, in fact, only pay Jay on a part-time basis. The congregation collaborated with their ecosystem of partners to launch Lattice Ministries as a 501(c)3. In this way, they could raise funds for the community hub that the campus was becoming. While Jay hoped that a path for New Hope Presbyterian's ongoing presence on campus would emerge with time, he coached the congregation to hold long-term outcomes loosely and to keep returning to the question, "How does the church become the heart of the community?"

When the COVID-19 pandemic took a considerable toll on the aging congregation, New Hope Presbyterian leaders eventually determined it was time to close or engraft in another congregation. Choosing to engraft that they might maintain their relationships with one another, New Hope Presbyterian and the presbytery ensured that the typical path of engrafting—in which the receiving church can sell or use the incoming church's property—would not take place. Lattice Ministries would support the worshiping communities, nonprofit organizations, and recreation groups continuing to create a place of belonging on campus. Adlin, who stays connected to Lattice Ministries through volunteering and giving, says of the time, "I knew I was going to miss New Hope Presbyterian. But because I was maturing in my faith and soul, I knew [engrafting] was the right thing to do."

While there was much to grieve with the departure of New Hope from campus, the former members continue to take pride in the vision of a Ruth community that lives on through Lattice Ministries. Ninety-year-old Kay muses that Lattice Ministries "is how God saw to complete the mission of the Presbyterian church."

New Hope Presbyterian members risked belonging to the neighborhood in which they were located. They risked caring more about the neighborhood than about their own preservation. They dared to imagine that God would be with them no matter what at the end of it all. As a result, they were able to help give birth, in Pastor Thang's words, to "a piece of heaven already. . . . [This is a place] of loving all those different groups of people, different languages, different cultures, where you are preparing yourself for heaven."

The Practice of Subversive Belonging

Amid societal, communal, and institutional changes, the throughline of New Hope Presbyterian Church's story is resurrection. A congregation in decline was revived by the Spirit's work, knitting relationships across so many lines of difference. Embracing an ethic of risk, the community gave birth to what is today a flourishing hub where newcomers and established Americans can worship, play, and learn to belong to one another.

In its final decade, the New Hope Presbyterian congregation participated in the formation of a community that, despite its limited size and budget, did not shy away from addressing the crisis of forced displacement that was reshaping their neighborhood. Instead, they learned to respond interpersonally, through the sharing of meals, and organizationally, through the sharing of sanctuaries, offices, and campus grounds. The community also learned to respond politically, with some members of the congregation drawn into the work of advocating for more just immigration and integration policies. The New Hope Presbyterian congregation dared to expand the boundaries of their belonging to include neighbors whose different racial, religious, cultural, and socioeconomic backgrounds are often systematically demarcated as "other" in this country.[7] In so doing, the church learned what it meant to become the heart of the community, even as their ability to remain in that community became uncertain.

New Hope Presbyterian members risked defining faithfulness in terms of the quality of their relationships with God, God's people, and the place in which they found themselves. The story of New Hope Presbyterian Church invites congregations to embrace an ethic of risk and to challenge traditional boundaries of belonging in their neighborhoods. Amid a rapidly changing religious landscape, we cannot begin to imagine what God is going to do through our faith communities in the seasons ahead. The experiences of the New Hope Presbyterian community remind us, however, that God's Spirit goes with us as we risk belonging to our communities and bear witness to the possibilities of resurrection.

Bibliography

Powell, John, and Stephen Menendian. *Belonging Without Othering: How We Save Ourselves and the World*. Redwood City, CA: Stanford University Press, 2024.

Welch, Sharon D. *A Feminist Ethic of Risk*. Minneapolis: Fortress, 2000.

7. Powell and Menendian, *Belonging Without Othering*, 18.

PART 6
Creation

Chapter 17

On Seeing and Being Seen
Holy Portraits, Presence, and Belonging

JENNIFER AWES FREEMAN

ON THE FIRST DAY of the term, I often begin class—regardless of teaching context—with an exercise I refer to simply as the "no-look portrait."[1] First, students divide themselves up into pairs and turn to face each other. With a piece of paper and a writing utensil, they begin to draw their partner—without ever looking down at what they're drawing. In theory, this exercise can encourage "close-looking" skills, as the inability to look down at one's paper forces concentration on (or at least, a heightened awareness of) the physical connection between the act of viewing a subject and attempting to create representative lines. I instruct students to pay attention to the contours of their partner's face and the relationship of its various parts: *Where does the eyebrow end? How does it relate to the curve of the temple, the cheekbone? Think three-dimensionally, topographically. Imagine your pen tracing the contour of the face, the rise of the nose's bridge, the valley at the edge of the mouth.* (I also suggest that students refrain from lifting their pens from the paper and thus losing their spots—which would guarantee a Picasso-like outcome!) Suddenly, the medieval understanding of the eyeball as an active, probing organ that extends into the world "touching"

---

1. Nicolaides, *Natural Way to Draw*, 5–14.

what it views seems very possible and present as students squint and stare at each other with intense effort.[2]

At a basic level, this exercise serves as an effective icebreaker—especially for undergraduate classrooms. Many students are nervous to draw, let alone to draw someone they just met; giggling often punctuates the silence of their concentration. When time is up and the students share their drawings with each other, there is more laughter and commiseration. But there is also encouragement, as students charitably point out the successes of their peers, however minimal and abstracted.

When I offer this exercise in a seminary classroom, I conclude it by inviting students to reflect on how the "no-look drawing" might relate to the practice of presence in their respective vocations. I suggest that the act of focusing on their partner—often in awkward silence, observing the details of their faces and expression and thus their particularity—is akin to the work of pastoral or spiritual care. In such ministerial work, *seeing* another person and being *present* with them is essential. This practice can also be understood as foundational to the personal humility and affirmation of others' dignity that is required for authentic hospitality and service to neighbors, as well as for spiritual exercises like prayer and meditation, because, in the words of Simone Weil, "attention, taken to the highest degree, is the same thing as prayer. It presupposes faith and love."[3] That is, it assumes that there is something worth attending to (and therefore worth all the time and energy that might require).

I share this example not just to recommend a playful exercise to the reader (which I heartily do!), but more importantly to suggest that portraiture as an artistic genre has the potential for profound theological and spiritual meaning. Indeed, the "holy portrait" has a deep history in Christian art and theology, founded on at least two key premises: 1) that humans are created in the image of God and 2) that the material world is ultimately *good*, and therefore both can communicate something of the divine. In what follows, I hope to highlight what I take to be significant theological and ethical imperatives that can be gleaned from the artistic tradition of icons and their theology (i.e., iconology). In this time of increased political and social polarization within the United States, as well as numerous international wars, famines, and pandemics, a personal commitment to embodied presence, slow-looking (i.e., careful observation),

---

2. Biernoff, *Sight and Embodiment*.
3. Weil, "Attention and Will," 212.

and sitting with the particularities of another person is a small but radical act that has the potential to affirm the humanity of others and ultimately build communities of belonging.

Icons and Iconology

The word "icon"[4] in its art historical usage refers to images of Jesus, Mary, and the saints that are used in Eastern Orthodox Christian devotion.[5] While most icons are panel paintings rendered with egg tempera and gold leaf, icons are found in other materials, ranging from mosaics to textiles, and technically speaking can be made in any medium. Icons are characterized by several common elements: the figures are depicted in either frontal facing or three-quarter views, and identifiable through accompanying labels or the attributes they carry. These subjects may be presented as busts or full-length figures, in non-narrative or narrative compositions. Portrayed with mouths closed and devoid of extreme emotion or drama, icons are, in a sense, silent and still. But theirs is not an empty silence; rather, it is an invitation for contemplation, whether of the life of the saint depicted (e.g., St. Olga), a biblical story (e.g., the Nativity), or the *imago Dei* in oneself. While religious images certainly have the capacity to instruct and inspire, icons in particular—through the visual elements just outlined—are relational in their presentation.

The Orthodox tradition is quick to clarify that the materials of wood and paint are not the object of veneration (i.e., honor); rather, the image by its very nature as *eikon* is a site of presence that directs the viewer elsewhere—such that icons are often referred to as "windows" or "doors" to heaven. This orientation towards the spiritual by means of the visual and material is reflected in the stylization of icons, which overall is flattened and abstracted. The figures tend to have large eyes and elongated features, and wear garments highlighted with geometric shapes like the facets of a jewel. The icon's architectural elements are completely unconcerned with the linear perspective of, say, the Italian Renaissance, because its goal is to point to a spiritual reality. Instead, icons employ an inverse perspective that converges on the viewer, implicitly inviting introspection.

---

4. The word "icon" is simply the cognate of its Greek origin *eikon*, which in its most basic sense is translated just as "image."

5. For an overview of Orthodox icons, see Ouspensky and Lossky, *Meaning of Icons*.

The icon offers the attentive viewer a point of encounter that traverses time and space. It brings the "cloud of witnesses" of the saints, matriarchs, and patriarchs into the present and, therefore, one of the most important contexts for the icon is that of communal worship. In an Orthodox Church, icons are found throughout the building, visualizing and reinforcing the theology of the liturgy: they are first encountered in the narthex (entryway) of the church, where icons of Mary and Jesus are typically displayed at the entrance of the nave (hall or "sanctuary") to be greeted with a kiss before entering (e.g., image 1).

Image 1: Narthex, Holy Trinity Orthodox Church, St. Paul, Minnesota (photo by Amanda Kroenig).

This and other postures of veneration (like bowing one's head) bring the person quite literally face to face with the icon. Murals often adorn the walls of the nave, featuring figures from the Hebrew Bible who have associations with covenant (e.g., Moses parting the Red Sea) or healing and salvation (e.g., Daniel in the Lion's Den).

Image 2: Nave mural, Holy Trinity Orthodox Church, St. Paul, Minnesota (photo by Amanda Kroenig).

There are typically three icon stands at the front of the church: a central stand featuring the festal icon (or patron saint of the church) and stands at the right and left featuring icons of Jesus and Mary respectively. Orthodox Christians venerate icons by crossing themselves, bowing, and then kissing or touching the icon; when a candle stand is available, they may also light candles.

The iconostasis,[6] punctured by three doors, bears images of the annunciation, the gospel writers, Jesus and Mary, the archangels Gabriel and Michael, and the patron saint(s) of the church.

Image 3: Iconostasis, Holy Trinity Orthodox Church, St. Paul, MN (photo by Amanda Kroenig).

An image of Mary with arms raised and the infant Jesus within a roundel on her chest (an incarnational motif known as "Our Lady of the Sign") usually adorns the curved wall of the apse directly above the altar. All of which is to say that in their liturgical context, icons immerse the congregation in the salvation narrative, as biblical figures, saints, and angels seem to stand around them, joining in the hymns of thanksgiving.

At several points during the liturgy of an Orthodox Christian Church, deacons cense the icons—as well as the congregation, because they too are icons of God. Likewise, an Orthodox funeral service concludes with the veneration of the body; the attendees line up at the open casket in the center of the church (i.e., where the central icon stand would otherwise be located) while the choir repeatedly sings "Memory eternal" and each person bows, touches, or kisses the body, venerating it as an image of God.

---

6. Literally "icon stand" or "icon screen," the iconostasis is a large structure that demarcates the nave from the altar.

Practices like these powerfully acknowledge and celebrate the human as an image of the divine.[7]

The liturgical context and the treatment (or "viewer reception") of icons is an important part of their identification as such. Though the earliest extant, identifiably Christian art dates to the late second century or early third century CE, the development of the icon as a distinct focus of prayer and site of holy presence does not seem to have emerged until the late sixth century, roughly contemporary to the advent of Islam.[8] The so-called iconoclastic controversy emerged in Byzantium during the eighth and ninth centuries around the scandal of whether humble materials like paint and wood could represent the divine nature of Jesus. The iconophile (literally "image-lover") position argued that it was precisely the incarnation that not only affirmed but *necessitated* portraits of Jesus. To deny such images was, in their mind, to deny the reality of the incarnation, that God became flesh and thus was particular and imageable.

It is not only the viewing of an icon that invites stillness, contemplation, and encounter: like the "no-look portrait" described at the start of this essay, painting or "writing"[9] an icon is itself an endeavor that should be approached with prayer and intention. The painter meditates on the image's subject throughout the process, allowing themself to be formed as much as they as the artist are forming the image.

Just as the icon may be considered a "window to heaven," it can likewise be understood to serve as a mirror—for the artist and viewer alike, in that it invites those who encounter it to see themselves in the icon, as reflective embodiments of the divine. It is precisely because icons strive to represent the image of God that their form and subject matter have the potential to invite or exclude. And so, conversely, these "windows" or "doors" to heaven can be experienced as closed to some based on whom they do *not* depict.

---

7. At home, Orthodox Christians typically have an "icon corner," that is, a corner or wall where several icons are displayed.

8. Jensen, *Understanding Early Christian Art*; *Emergence of Christian Devotional Images*; Brubaker, *Inventing Byzantine Iconoclasm*.

9. Because icons are understood to be a distinct theological language, their creation is often referred to as "writing."

PART 6: CREATION

Icons Reimagined

While the Orthodox tradition of icons, which spans about fifteen hundred years, consists of various styles ascribed to distinct "schools" (e.g., Novgorod, Athos, Ethiopian, Coptic), its theology, materials, and subject matter remain largely consistent, having become increasingly codified in the aftermath of the Triumph of Orthodoxy in 843.[10] In recent decades, the icon as an art form has gained wider awareness and interest from Orthodox and non-Orthodox alike. Newer generations of artists are extending and reimagining what the icon is and can be. For example, the Ukrainian iconographer Ivanka Demchuk paints in a modern minimalist style that (in this author's opinion) still expresses the spirit of the tradition. Many non-Orthodox people have encountered the icon through iconography workshops, as for example, the Prosopon School of Iconology, founded by Vladislav Andrejev, focuses on the theology (iconology) and spiritual practice of icon writing. The school welcomes students of any or no religious identity to participate in their intensive courses.

Some Catholic iconographers have contributed to the increased incorporation of icons into Catholic contexts, and artists like Robert Lentz (of the Order of the Friars Minor)[11] have celebrated more recent historical figures whose lives resonate with the Catholic Social Gospel, such as Cesar Chavez, Simone Weil, and Martin Luther King Jr., through their rendering in icons. That is, the icon as a kind of honorific artform has the capacity to make an argument for re/considering someone as a spiritual—and social—model. Lentz has also created icons of Jesus as a Black man and as an Indigenous man.

Father William McNichols, known to many as Fr. Bill, studied iconography under Robert Lentz in the 1990s after many years of serving AIDS patients in hospice care at the peak of the crisis in New York City and as an out gay Catholic priest.[12] Like his teacher, Fr. Bill has created images of saints past and present, and has elevated the marginalized with his paintbrush, honoring the dignity of AIDS patients, as well as Matthew Shepherd and others (e.g., image 4).

---

10. The Triumph of Orthodoxy refers to the official ending of the Byzantine iconoclastic controversy.
11. Lentz and Gateley, *Christ in the Margins*.
12. Pramuk and McNichols, *All My Eyes See*.

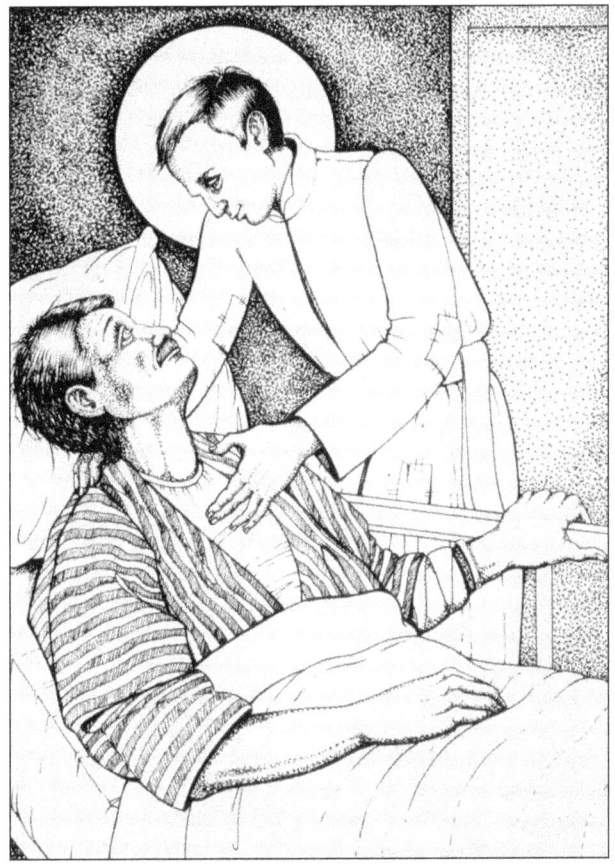

Image 4: *St. Aloysius Visiting a Person with AIDS,* William Hart McNichols, 1986 © William Hart McNichols (*FrBillMcNichols-SacredImages.com*).

Mark Doox's iconographic work perhaps became most widely known through the viral sharing of his 2015 painting *Our Lady, Mother of Ferguson and All Those Killed by Gun Violence* (known also as *Our Lady of Ferguson*), commissioned by the Rev. Dr. Mark Francisco Bozzuti-Jones to commemorate the killing of Michael Brown. Though Doox had learned to paint traditional icons as a novice monk at an Orthodox monastery in Texas decades earlier, his iconographic calling, so to speak, came after he had left the monastery and was invited to paint an icon of John Coltrane for the Saint John Coltrane Church in San Francisco in the early 1990s. He then worked on an icon program at the church over the next several years. From 1998 to 2008, Doox painted the rotunda of St. Gregory of

Nyssa Orthodox Church in San Francisco with rows of dancing saints, interspersed from across the centuries, including Rumi, Ella Fitzgerald, Andrei Rublev, Charles Darwin, Black Elk, Archbishop Desmond Tutu, and even a few animals, like Francis of Assisi's wolf.[13]

Over the years, Doox has developed a distinct style, coined "Byz-Dada" (i.e., Byzantine Dada), which employs Byzantine style and iconography to visualize satirically the history and current reality of being Black in America (e.g., image 5).

Image 5: *St. John Coltrane Enthroned (Alabama),* Mark Doox, 2020.

This development has culminated in the recent publication of Doox's book, *The N-Word of God*, which is "a literary graphic novel and art book of interconnected illustrated stories of social insight, cognitive surprise, wry mirth and black existential wonder. By appropriating Christian iconography

13. SGNEC, "Fifteen Years of Dancing with the Saints."

and recontextualizing daring American terms and caricatures, Doox creates symbols of resilience, relevant insight, sly protection, and revelation pertinent to all."[14] The visual effect of the book is nothing short of explosively kaleidoscopic—a descent into the layered iconography of capitalism, white supremacy, and Christianity that offers a way through (if not out) by the inversion, and sometimes collapsing, of binaries.

The Russian-born and now Oregon-based artist Olga Volchkova was traditionally trained as an iconographer, but now applies those artistic methods and iconography to deify flora and fauna instead of people. One series presents personifications of various plants, such as Saint Saffron, Saint Oak, and Saint Belladonna (e.g., image 6).

Image 6: *St. Belladonna,* Olga Volchkova, 2012.

14. Doox, *N-Word of God*, back cover.

The images are often bust portraits, frontal facing, and nimbed with traditional gold haloes or auras created by natural elements like flowers or dandelion puffs. They are situated in natural and architectural environments alike, often with rich decorative borders that include flowers and fruit. They are identified accordingly with red name titles or scrolls of text. Volchkova's work extends belonging and community to the natural and animal world, thereby inviting the viewer to "consider the lilies of the field" (Matthew 6:28) not as mere ornament, but as divine neighbor.

Conclusion: Looking Outward, Looking Forward

Since its earliest manifestations, Christian art has translated the Christian story into a visual vocabulary that is legible to the community and time for which it was made—whether the clean-shaven toga-clad Jesus of the Roman catacombs, the red-bearded Jesus of the Book of Kells, or the evangelist Mark of the Garima Gospels who sits in a leopard-print chair and composes in Ge'ez. Contemporary icons by artists like Fr. Bill and Mark Doox also traverse time by bringing their biblical and historical subjects into the present. By visually translating the gospel message, they question who it is that "belongs" and thus ultimately expand and celebrate the "cloud of witnesses."

When considered in its historic and contemporary contexts, the holy portrait is both a confrontation and an invitation. It affirms the essential goodness of humanity and creation—the divine in all people, and thus challenges any death-dealing theology and politics that reject, deny, and exclude. The holy portrait embraces creativity, beauty, and wonder as legitimate vocabularies for theology and ethics. As a site of presence and encounter, it asks the viewer for slow-looking, a practice of presence, and the willingness to be transformed. This transformation does not occur in a vacuum or merely on an individual, internal level. Rather, the portrait is holy in that it can help us to recognize the divine in our neighbor—and calls us to respond accordingly in the world.

Bibliography

Biernoff, Suzannah. *Sight and Embodiment in the Middle Ages.* New York: Palgrave Macmillan, 2002.

Brubaker, Leslie. *Inventing Byzantine Iconoclasm.* London: Bristol Classical, 2011.

Doox, Mark. *The N-Word of God.* Seattle: Fantagraphics, 2024.

Jensen, Robin M. *From Idols to Icons: The Emergence of Christian Devotional Images in Late Antiquity.* Oakland: University of California Press, 2022.

———. *Understanding Early Christian Art.* 2nd ed. New York: Routledge, 2024.

Lentz, Robert, and Edwina Gateley. *Christ in the Margins.* Maryknoll, NY: Orbis, 2003.

Nicolaïdes, Kimon. *The Natural Way to Draw: A Working Plan for Art Study.* Boston: Houghton Mifflin, 1941.

Ouspensky, Leonid, and Vladimir Lossky. *The Meaning of Icons.* 2nd ed. Yonkers: St. Vladimir's, 1999.

Pramuk, Christopher, and William Hart McNichols. *All My Eyes See: The Artistic Vocation of Fr. William Hart McNichols.* Maryknoll, NY: Orbis, 2024.

Saint Gregory of Nyssa Episcopal Church (SGNEC). "Fifteen Years of Dancing with the Saints." n.d. https://saintgregorys.org/dancing-saints.

Weil, Simone. "Attention and Will." In *Simone Weil: An Anthology*, edited by Sian Miles, 211–17. New York: Grove, 1986.

Chapter 18

Voice and Verse

Breathing and Belonging Together

CRAIG LEMMING

> Blest pair of Sirens, pledges of Heav'ns joy,
> Sphear-born harmonious Sisters, Voice, and Vers,
> Wed your divine sounds, and mixt power employ
> Dead things with inbreath'd sense able to pierce,
> And to our high-rais'd phantasie present,
> That undisturbèd Song of pure content,
> Ay sung before the saphire-colour'd throne
> To him that sits theron
> With Saintly shout, and solemn Jubily,
> Where the bright Seraphim in burning row
> Their loud up-lifted Angel trumpets blow,
> And the Cherubick host in thousand quires
> Touch their immortal Harps of golden wires,
> With those just Spirits that wear victorious Palms,
> Hymns devout and holy Psalms
> Singing everlastingly;
> That we on Earth with undiscording voice
> May rightly answer that melodious noise;
> As once we did, till disproportion'd sin
> Jarr'd against natures chime, and with harsh din

Broke the fair musick that all creatures made
To their great Lord, whose love their motion sway'd
In perfect Diapason, whilst they stood
In first obedience, and their state of good.
O may we soon again renew that Song
And keep in tune with Heav'n, till God ere long
To his celestial consort us unite,
To live with him, and sing in endles morn of light.[1]

I FIRST SANG THESE words in the early 1990s as a boy treble standing next to my mother in the parish choir of Saint Elizabeth of Hungary Anglican Church in Harare, Zimbabwe. It was a concert of sacred music that culminated in our singing of Sir Charles Hubert Hastings Parry's breathtaking setting of Milton's *At a Solemn Musick*.[2] One might wonder why an adolescent, "colored"[3] boy was singing Edwardian choral music composed by his racist Anglican colonizers in independent Zimbabwe. Surely hit songs by Boyz II Men, Oliver Mtukudzi, or Mariah Carey should have had a far greater appeal and influence on his musical tastes and interests. My family's racial mixedness and in-betweenness in post-apartheid Southern Africa placed us in what Gloria E. Anzaldúa called "the borderlands"[4]—liminal spaces occupied by inconvenient peoples, like us, whose very being defies, disobeys, and disrupts the neat, racialized categories invented by Western European and Anglo North Atlantic colonizers. Yes, that twelve-year-old colored boy who sang the fussiest *fioritura* in Handel arias could also keep up with Whitney Houston's most elaborate of spellbinding riffs honed in the Black Church.

As I ponder what belonging means for fellow Borderland Peoples whose bodies are thresholds of "both/and-ness," this meditation is about communal singing as a spirit-based practice that cultivates kinship across our many lines of difference.

---

1. Milton, "At a Solemn Musick," 157–58.
2. See Bournemouth Symphony Orchestra, "Blest Pair of Sirens—Parry."
3. "Colored" refers to the racial class imposed upon people of mixed race in Southern Africa.
4. Anzaldua, *Borderlands/La Frontera*.

PART 6: CREATION

Perhaps that ancient, human desire to express truths in poetry that flows on the breath we share as we sing together is a place to begin doing both the inner and outer work of racial healing. In our breathing and singing we literally conspire to create beauty, truth, and goodness. In our minds we aspire to Milton's dizzying heights of reconciliation with God, neighbors, and all of creation. In our bodies we are inspired, despite our heartbreak, to continue fighting for those who can't breathe.

Breathing in, thinking, and singing words of faith, hope, and love as one body can create belonging for all bodies. Like Milton, I believe those sphere-born harmonious sisters, Voice and Verse, still wed their divine sounds through communal singing. By trusting in that mixed power of words and music married in our mixed voices, our singing might redeem the interdependent, multicultural human belonging that racist colonizers try to kill. I believe that when voices of all peoples sing divine words together, that "inbreathed sense able to pierce" breaks hardened hearts, converts ossified minds, and heals wounded souls.

Isn't this, after all, why singing has been integral to all revolutionary acts of love and liberation? From the biblical canticle of Miriam (Exod 15:20-27) to the prison-bursting hymns of Paul and Silas (Acts 16:25-26). From the liberation-encoded spirituals of enslaved African peoples to the PRIDE anthems of Gloria Gaynor and Sylvester that have consoled, strengthened, and sustained LGBTQ+ communities. Singing together creates inclusive belonging in those places and spaces that white supremacist culture tries and fails to make demonically exclusive.

Before Jesus suffered his agony in the garden of Gethsemane, we read in the Gospel of Matthew, "When they had sung the hymn, they went out to the Mount of Olives" (Matt 26:30). Jesus and his followers sang together on the night the birth pangs of the redemption of the universe began. I wonder what words, melodies, and harmonies they sang in that upper room? What did that community of voices sound like when they sang that hymn together? Was it raucous and celebratory? Was it hushed and contemplative? Perhaps it was a heady mixture of love and terror. That mixed power of hope and fear that is unmistakable in voices of the oppressed singing for freedom. From the Jim Crow South to apartheid South Africa, peoples in the borderlands and on the margins have kept singing of love and liberty for all. Even though their voices shook, they created shared musical language of pluriversal belonging.

Mary the mother of Jesus sang her *Magnificat* while pregnant with God's Redeeming Love (Luke 1:46–55). In phrases that juxtapose our human extremities, Mary's adolescent voice and verse hold them together in divine paradox: magnificence and lowliness; might and mercy; put-downs and exaltations; fullness and emptiness. Did Mary teach her song to her son? Did Jesus sing her *Magnificat*? In his fully human and fully divine mixedness and in-between-ness, what did Jesus's voice sound like? A plaintive tenor, mellow bass-baritone, or perhaps an otherworldly, androgynous countertenor? I wonder whether the mixed power of those words and music in the hymn they sang together on the night Jesus was betrayed resulted in three-day earworms—phrases of a song that get stuck in our memory, that refuse to be forgotten, sung internally over and over again, that make us relive the timeless moment we first heard or sang them.

As we reckon with post-George Floyd revelations of this world's far-too-long legacy of racialized trauma, betrayals, tortures, and crucifixions, what sacred earworms might we start co-creating by singing together? What sacred words and music will get stuck in your mind's ear and haunt the memories of your children's children? Is this not the meaning of Christ's *Anamnesis*: to refuse to forget who and whose we are by re-membering Christ's broken body and blood poured out for all creation to be healed?

As my heart breaks in the wake of ceaseless cruelty that racist violence produces, I often hear Parry's agonizing dissonance composed to express that "disproportioned sin" that jars "with a harsh din" against the tender, interdependent harmony of Creation's web. The relationship-distorting sin of racism breaks the music all creatures are made to create together to the Holy One, the one who laid the earth's cornerstone when the morning stars sang together and all the heavenly beings shouted for joy (Job 38:7). In my reflexive work as a practical theologian of intersecting, mixed, marginalized identities, I strive to infuse my priestly ministry with Gloria Anzaldúa's concept of "*las nepantleras*"—those whom she describes as "threshold people" who "move within and among multiple worlds and use their movement in the service of transformation."[5] As a priest creating sacred spaces and sacramental rituals for people of all demographic differences to commune together with God in the reconciling love of Christ, Anzaldúa's words strike a chord that resonates with my life's vocation:

> In gatherings where people feel powerless, *la nepantlera* offers rituals to say good-bye to old ways of relating; prayers to thank

---

5. Anzaldua, *Light in the Dark/Luz en Lo Oscuro*, xxxv.

life for making us face loss, anger, guilt, fear, and separation; *rezos* to acknowledge our individual wounds; and commitments to not give up on others just because they hurt us. In gatherings where we've forgotten that the object of conflict is peace, *la nepantlera* proposes spiritual techniques (mindfulness, openness, receptivity) along with activist tactics. Where before we saw only separateness, differences, and polarities, our connectionist sense of spirit recognizes nurturance and reciprocity and encourages alliances among groups working to transform communities. In gatherings where we feel our dreams have been sucked out of us, *la nepantlera* leads us in celebrating *la comunidad soñada*, reminding us that spirit connects the irreconcilable warring parts *para que todo el mundo se haga un paíz*, so that the whole world may become *un pueblo*.[6]

Creating places and spaces in which Anzaldúa's "dream community" of multiple human identities can thrive together invites us to imagine how our structures of belonging might be infused with an Anzaldúan celebration of in-between-ness. The challenging requirement of belonging in such a community, just the way we are, is the shared responsibility of making enough room for others to belong, too, just the way they are. Can the songs we sing together invite each person to be fully themselves in the presence of God? Does the music we make communally as people of God make us desire to belong in-between one another's distinctive identities? Do we make music steeped in structures of mutual and reciprocal trust?

The discomfort of in-between-ness teaches us the meaning of mutuality and reciprocity. This delicate balance of mutual and reciprocal trust is cultivated in ensemble singing. If I sing what is sacred to you, with you, will you sing what is sacred to me, with me? And as we sing together, in-between our respective interiority and exteriority, a reflective examen begins to shape a keen self-awareness. Am I too loud? Am I loud enough? If I can't hear their voice over mine, are they singing loud enough, or am I being insensitive? Is my voice being overwhelmed by theirs? While I have a great reverence for the sound of perfectly blended voices honed to perfection by Midwestern choirs, the style of ensemble singing I find more thrilling are groups of singers who are not trying to blend at all. Instead, they allow their distinctive voice to be heard among other equally distinctive voices as they each make room for one another's unique vocal colors, timbres, and styles to shimmer. Voices, like fingerprints, are created to be one-of-a-kind, so trying to sound exactly the same as the voices next to

---

6. Anzaldua, *Light in the Dark/Luz en Lo Oscuro*, 149.

yours compromises what Howard Thurman calls "the sound of the genuine in you."[7] Yes, we still do our utmost to sing in tune, on time, and within a shared dynamic range, but the authenticity of our particular voice's distinctive color palette is relished best when all the particular characteristics of our voices are free to sound completely genuine.

What I love most about singing in choirs and congregations are those moments when we look into one another's faces, truly see one another's differences, take collective breaths, and trust that that sound of our shared humanity emerging from our mixed vocal timbres creates the realities our sacred words describe. That the time and space around us will resonate with imagery, consonance, dissonance, and resolutions that transform us. That moment of collective trust is what faith feels like. An instant when our imaginations are completely focused on co-creating beauty, truth, and goodness together, literally out of thin air. It is a profound feeling to know our particular voice not only belongs but is essential to enriching an interdependent trust in one another's participation with the Holy Spirit. In this way, making all that is, seen and unseen, new.

We cannot measure this phenomenon. We cannot bottle it up or preserve it. It defies mass production and commodification. Those times of profound trust in belonging to one another in collective singing is a palpable reality experienced in unrepeatable moments of suddenly being in tune with what Milton calls the "perfect Diapason" of God's creative love. In this historical moment of profound discord, isolation, and broken trust, maybe the spiritual discipline of singing sacred songs with those who differ most from us is one small yet powerful starting point. Even if our voices shake, we practice this trust and choose to belong to one another. With each collective breath and phrase we sing together, we glimpse God's reconciling love as our hearts, minds, bodies, and spirits synchronize.

According to John 20:21–22, the resurrected Christ says to his followers, "Peace be with you. As the Creator has sent me, so I send you." When Jesus said this, he breathed on them and said to them, "Receive the Holy Spirit." As we breathe in and receive the Holy Spirit of Jesus, what we choose to do with that collective breath is a gift. The gift of belonging to each other, in between one another's differences, and belonging to God altogether are realities as close as our next breath. Whether it's Parry or Prince, when we choose to sing to God with neighbors who differ most from us, we all suddenly belong.

7. Thurman, "Sound of the Genuine."

PART 6: CREATION

Bibliography

Anzaldua, Gloria E. *Borderlands/La Frontera: The New Mestiza.* San Francisco: Aunt Lute, 1999.

———. *Light in the Dark/Luz en Lo Oscuro: Rewriting Identity, Spirituality, Reality.* Durham: Duke University Press, 2015.

Bournemouth Symphony Orchestra. "Blest Pair of Sirens—Parry." *YouTube*, June 10, 2011. https://youtu.be/gHNvJsGXDjc?.

Milton, John. "At a Solemn Musick." In *The Complete Poetry of John Milton*, edited by John T. Shawcross, 157–58. New York: Doubleday, 1963.

Thurman, Howard. "The Sound of the Genuine." Baccalaureate Ceremony at Spelman College, May 4, 1980. Howard Thurman Digital Archive. https://thurman.pitts.emory.edu/items/show/838.

Chapter 19

Cultural Humility as a Pathway to Belonging

B. Hunter Farrell

The Cost of Belonging

I REMEMBER VIVIDLY THE day Congolese Pastor Kashama gently challenged my somewhat simplistic understanding of what it means to belong. I had lived in Congo for about a year and was learning Tshiluba, a Congolese language deeply sensitive to the nuance of kinship and belonging. As we walked toward the Kananga city market on a busy sidewalk, I practiced my greeting with everyone I passed, *Wetu'au muan'etu*! (literally, "This person is our sibling!"). The greeting serves as a clearer marker of kinship, of belonging, to be sure, but also the weighty responsibility that creates. Pastor Kashama stopped me and said, "To greet someone as sibling means you'll share with them whatever you have." I was dumbfounded. I must admit my first thought was more about my bank account and medical insurance than about any sense of connection with Congolese neighbors. But Pastor Kashama was right: belonging carries a high cost.

Sociologists and social psychologists have long noted that US society distinguishes itself by being the most individualistic in the world. Many Africans (and Middle Easterners, Asians, and Latin Americans—in fact, most of the world) understand their identity as "we" and not "me" and draw their sense of identity from their extended family, as exemplified in the well-known notion of *ubuntu*: "I am because we are." At the other end of the cultural continuum, those of us—particularly Whites/Euro-Americans—formed primarily by the American cultural streams of individualized human rights and rugged individualism find ourselves alone, imagining ourselves as primarily responsible for the decisions that will shape our life.

Even our economic system pushes us to live as islands of individuality: we are conditioned daily to separate ourselves from others and to consume alone. Princeton sociologist Robert Putnam's book, *Bowling Alone*, observed that Americans increasingly *bowl alone*—that the social capital that has bound us together throughout our history is quickly eroding. We increasingly eat, drink, vacation, retire, and die alone. Thus, in the US, the notion of belonging has fallen on hard times because it represents an almost scandalous challenge to the individualized self-actualization which has become the bright, rising moon that many of us worship.

Of course, many of us long for relationship, for community, for a sense of belonging. We ache through the loneliness and isolation that come with self-reliance. We yearn for the warmth of knowing and being known. Yet we are also innately aware of the *cost of belonging*—what we must give up to be part of something greater. An example from the realm of international politics: when a country signs a defense treaty, it binds itself to other countries whose choices it cannot control. An attack against any of the treaty signers is considered an attack on my own country. A country must renounce a portion of its own sovereignty in order to gain a measure of protection against a perceived common threat. Part of the cost of belonging is that I am forced to acknowledge the limitations of *me*: my sovereignty, my independence, my coveted preferences.

A Parable of Belonging

New revelations about the power and fragility of belonging often come in the form of ordinary experiences and ordinary stories. An image. An encounter. A phrase. These are the spaces in time that invite us to see our belonging in a new way.

Scriptures frequently present these encounters in parables. Lutheran New Testament scholar Mark Allen Powell tells of the cultural lenses through which we "see" Scripture.[1] Powell asked a diverse group

---

1. Powell, *What Do They Hear?*, 247.

of Americans, Russians, and Tanzanians to read the story of the prodigal son in Luke 15 and to retell it from memory to another person. After the exercise, he posed the question, "Why did the younger son go hungry?" The responses were surprising: 100 percent of the Americans said that the son had squandered his inheritance. 84 percent of the Russians said it was "because of the famine" (almost no American recalled the famine). Most of the Tanzanians said it was because "no one gave him anything to eat." Across many sub-Saharan African communities, it is considered shameful for a community to allow a member to go hungry.

Powell then looked back at what the text actually says. In verse 13, it says the prodigal son "squandered his wealth." In verse 14, it attributes his hunger to "a famine in the land." In verse 16, it states that "no one gave him anything to eat." All three interpretations were essentially correct, but all three were incomplete. The Americans stressed individual responsibility. The Russians' cultural memory of food shortages and famine is so present that they *couldn't not* feel empathy for the hungry young man. The Tanzanians understood innately that we owe it to each other to keep each other from starving.

But the main point of the parable is not *how* the young man got into trouble, but that the loving father drops everything to race toward his son and embrace him. Could it be that all of us are minority shareholders in the truth and that we need each other to complete our partial understanding? That *my* knowledge of God needs to be completed by *yours*? Could it be that none of us knows how to love completely, but that we learn to love *together*?

This is the power of belonging: our eyes are opened to the fact that we need each other to make sense of the world. Certainly, "many hands make light work," as the proverb says—we're stronger together than we are alone. But there is something deeper at work when we perceive the sense of belonging this interpretive exercise presents: when our eyes are opened to the reality of our shared connection, that our lives are knit together, we are gifted with the capacity to *de-center* ourselves—our self-justifying narratives, our limited notions of mystery, our blind spots. We are obligated to acknowledge the limited nature of our wisdom and are freed to *re-member* (i.e., *put back together, restore to relationship*) the Body of Christ, reconnecting what our hubris divided. The apostle Paul risked the wrath of the proud Corinthian church when he argued that "God chose what is foolish in the world to shame the wise, God chose what is weak in the world to shame the strong, God chose what is low and despised in the world, even the things that are not, to bring to nothing the things that are, so that no human being might boast in the presence of God" (1 Cor 1:27-29).

Peruvian liberation theologian Gustavo Gutiérrez once reflected in a Holy Week course for *agentes pastorales* in Lima, Peru that, while God loves all people, it is God's *amor peculiar*—that "peculiar love" that Gutierrez names as God's preferential option for the poor—that upends the world's hierarchies and supremacies, whether White, Hutu, Afrikaner, Israeli or other.[2]

But as a frequent flier on the airline of global privilege, I immediately sense the looming cost inherent in binding myself to what I perceive to be a world of need. In the Gospels, I'm wary when Jesus points out in Matthew that it is the elder brother's sense of birthright-privilege that blinds him to the reality that he and his wayward younger brother are bound together. In Luke, the Pharisee's spiritual resumé, carefully constructed over years of righteous works, distorts his vision causing him to stand apart from the sinful tax collector and see him as "other." Luke's parable of Lazarus and the rich man notes that not even the beggar's daily cries for food at the rich man's gate could cause the rich man to imagine sharing anything in common with Lazarus. Each of these Gospel cameos proffers the hope of belonging, but in each case, the cost of losing social, spiritual or economic privilege derails the protagonist's movement toward belonging. Like the elder son, the Pharisee, and the rich man, I remain in my gated community attempting in vain to thrive alone. Though our hearts long to live out the kind of belonging that brings us together as the human family, the cost frightens me. How might we find the courage to risk the promise of belonging?

Cultural Humility: A First Step Toward Belonging

Indeed it takes courage to create connections and community across the cultural divides of our highly diverse, yet stubbornly segregated, world: to count the cost of belonging and commit to earnestly seek it. What steps can we take to approach the embrace of belonging to people different from ourselves?

Through living and working in four languages on as many continents, I am learning that the first step in the path toward belonging is

2. Gutierrez, "Holy Week Short Course for Pastoral Agents."

cultivating the spirit and practices of cultural humility. Jesus's requirement that we "become as a child" to enter the realm of God touches the very heart of the challenge before us: we long ago outgrew a child's sense of wonder and the capacity to say, *I don't know*. We are constrained by an adult sense of responsibility that ages us until we find it difficult to enter the supple posture of a learner.

We need cultural humility because the cultural chasm that separates us from people whose gender identity, religious orientation, race, ability, or education differ from our own is multidimensional: individualistic vs. collectivistic, hierarchical vs. egalitarian, direct vs. indirect communication, long- vs. short-term orientation, and many more. Cultural patterns powerfully shape our assumptions and practices because they are *implicit*—rarely does anyone instruct us in how to greet someone (e.g., do we convey a sense of belonging by shaking with the right hand? a kiss on the right cheek? a deferential bow? engaging or avoiding direct eye contact?), but you're sure to hear about it if you do it wrong!

For people around the world, the path toward a sense of belonging is littered with misunderstandings and conflict generated by cultural differences. But Euro-Americans and Europeans face an additional challenge: the lens through which we see the world is shaped by a combination of cultural and historical factors that can derail our best intentions to communicate effectively and respectfully with others. Culturally speaking, because we tend to be extremely individualistic, direct communicators who lean decidedly toward short-term solutions, we can come off as abrupt and insensitive list-makers, rather than human beings who desire relationship. These cultural tendencies join with the tragic and enduring historical legacy of settler colonialism to introduce a Trojan horse of toxic assumptions of white supremacy with its *white savior* narrative into our collective imagination. This supremacist worldview profoundly distorts how we navigate cultural differences. Ironically, in our moment of greatest need for others, we tend to assume that we have the answers to their deepest questions. We fail to recognize that the potential blessing of belonging to persons with perspectives and insights quite different from our own far outweighs the cost of a loss of perceived privilege or sovereignty.

Wherever we stand in relation to the colonial legacy, cultural humility offers us a way to recognize and come together in belonging. As Tervalon and Murray-García first stated in their research on the power dynamics of the physician-patient encounter, cultural humility is born out of an understanding of intercultural encounter as an ongoing process built on practices of "self-reflection and self-critique as lifelong learners and reflective practitioners."[3] Cultural humility is not merely a one-dimensional competency that is mastered in an online learning module; rather, it is an attitude of deep respect for the other's personhood in the particularities of their difference that motivates us to develop a set of specific skills through a regular rhythm of curiosity for the other and disciplined self-reflection.

Cultural humility requires learners to notice and attend to the power imbalances intrinsic to human relationships, whether between physicians and patients, teachers and students, or documented citizens and undocumented laborers. We cannot pretend to come to the common table together unless we are prepared to acknowledge the power inequities that separate us and to commit to work on leaving them at the table, lest wealth-, race-, and gender-based hierarchies twist, distort and, ultimately, make a mockery of our attempts to recognize our human connectedness. The greater the power imbalance, that is, the greater our sense of privilege, the higher the cost of belonging. But a proverb from western Ethiopia reminds us that "we can only embrace with empty hands." Could it be that our deeply felt need to hold and be held can give us the courage to pay the price of belonging?

Cultural humility recognizes that every person brings to the table particular gifts, skills, insights and perspectives that the Body needs and thus opens up even the relatively powerful to the truth that they, too, belong to those they considered the "weaker" partner. The powerful Peruvian Catholic Church and a circle of NGOs brought resources, needed accompaniment and media savvy in support of the Andean city of La Oroya, Peru in its struggle against the illegal activities of a US smelting company that left a legacy of more than eight thousand lead-poisoned children. But the NGOs were surprised to learn of the greater power present in the community itself, where the authenticity of the local activists' first-person accounts eclipsed the power of all the statistics, third-person analyses and op-ed pieces the outsiders provided (it was *the people's story*, after all). This grand reversal of the traditional narrative of the center helping the periphery—of the powerful and educated saving the weak and less-educated—has been key in the various allies discovering a powerful sense of belonging.

In Colombia, Mennonites and Presbyterians publicly committed to accompany communities of former combatants of the Revolutionary Armed

---

3. Tervalon and Murray-Garcia, "Cultural Humility," 118.

Forces of Colombia[4] who, after sixty years of bloody conflict, laid down arms so that their children could have the chance to live in peace. The Colombian churches brought legitimacy and some resources to the former combatant communities committed to the peacemaking process, to be sure, but the experience is also permitting the former rebels to make an important contribution to the churches. In order to embrace the communities of former combatants, the churches have been required to pay a price: they have been confronted by the lived experience of people who broke laws, committed acts of violence, shunned religion, and set up an alternative society, all in the name of justice for the poor. "How can these lawbreakers deserve forgiveness?" not a few church members asked.

Yet the former combatants have stepped forward, pardons in hand, and seek to forge—non-violently now—a society which closely resembles the very realm of God that the church has been proclaiming for centuries! As the Colombian churches and former combatants spend time together, they engage in practices of cultural humility: understanding both their relationship and the peacemaking process as a long-term commitment that requires regular self-reflection and self-critique from the posture of a learner and naming and addressing the power dynamics which are present. These practices have allowed them to take the first steps to forge a deeper sense of belonging together. The cost to the churches has been high. But had they not found the courage to pay the price, they could not have experienced life in God's realm as they have. By *becoming as children* through practices of cultural humility, they have entered into God's realm in powerful ways.

By engaging in the attitudes and practices of cultural humility, all of us—even the "wise" or "powerful"—can receive the gift of new eyes to see that we belong to one another. By understanding the long-term, ongoing nature of our journey, by assuming the posture of a learner who engages in self-reflection and self-critique, and by acknowledging and responding to the power imbalances inherent in human relationships, we join Christ in the holy work of *re-membering* Christ's Body—restoring relationship with each other and with the God who reconciled us to Godself through Christ and gave us the ministry of reconciliation (2 Cor 5:18). In his reflection on "Unity, Not Uniformity," Malawian missiologist Harvey Collins Kwiyani asserts, "This walk of faith is a never-ending dance with strangers. In an

---

4. The Revolutionary Armed Forces of Columbia (FARC) fought against the government for more than sixty years. More than nine million people were killed in the violence.

absolute sense, in the Body of Christ, we are because we belong."[5] Cultural humility provides us with the space and the practices we need to dance together with strangers to whom we belong.

Bibliography

Farrell, B. Hunter, and S. Balajiedlang Khyllep. *Freeing Congregational Mission: A Practical Vision for Companionship, Cultural Humility, and Co-Development.* Downers Grove, IL: InterVarsity, 2022.

Gutierrez, Gustavo. "Holy Week Short Course for Pastoral Agents." Lima, Peru, April 6–10, 2000.

Kwiyani, Harvey Collins. *Decolonising Mission.* London: SCM, forthcoming.

Powell, Mark Allen. *What Do They Hear: Bridging the Gap Between Pulpit and Pew.* Nashville: Abingdon, 2007.

Putnam, Robert. *Bowling Alone: The Collapse and Revival of American Community.* New York: Simon & Schuster, 2000.

Tervalon, Melanie, and Jann Murray-Garcia. "Cultural Humility versus Cultural Competence: A Critical Distinction in Defining Physician Training Outcomes in Multicultural Settings." *Journal of Healthcare of the Poor and Underserved* 9 (1998) 117–25.

---

5. Kwiyani, *Decolonising Mission.*

Chapter 20

A Music-Making Counter-Community[1]

WALTER BRUEGGEMANN

AMONG THE MOST ELEGANT, wondrous prayers in *The Book of Common Prayer* is this one:

> O God, the creator and preserver of all mankind, we humbly beseech thee for all sorts and conditions of men; that thou wouldst be pleased to make thy ways known unto them, thy saving health unto all nations. More especially we pray for thy holy Church universal; that it may be so guided and governed by thy good Spirit, that all who profess and call themselves Christians may be led into the way of truth, and hold the faith in unity of spirit, in the bond of peace, and in righteousness of life. Finally, we commend to thy fatherly goodness all those who are in any ways afflicted or distressed, in mind, body, or estate; that it may please thee to comfort and relieve them according to their several necessities, giving them patience under their sufferings, and a happy issue out of all their afflictions. And this we beg for Jesus Christ's sake. Amen.[2]

The prayer includes petitions for "thy holy Church universal" and for all those "who are in any way afflicted or distressed in mind, body, or estate."

---

1. Used with permission. First published by *Church Anew*, May 2, 2023.
2. Episcopal Church, *Book of Common Prayer*, 814–15.

PART 6: CREATION

But the phrase that always brings me to a reflective pause is, "for all sorts and conditions of men." The phrase sweeps across class, race, nation, and ethnic origin. And while gender could not have been on the horizon of Thomas Cramner, it can readily and properly be added to the catalogue, as this prayer is cast in patriarchal terms. The prayer recognizes that a wide variety of human persons have a wide variety of needs about which to pray; but it also recognizes that in the presence of "the creator and preserver of all mankind," all of these different folk stand in common and shared need of providential care with the hope of "a happy issue" out of all affliction. It is a grand vision of shared humanity in its common vulnerability.

The phrasing of this prayer came to mind when my son, John, sent me an essay by Dave Hickey entitled, "Shining Hours/Forgiving Rhyme." It is from his collection entitled *Air Guitar*. In this brief essay Hickey recalls a Saturday morning when he was eight or nine years old. He remembers that he and his dad, who was going to play music, were "decked out in jazz-dude apparel: penny loafers, khakis, and Hawaiian shirts with the tails out."[3] They picked up a family friend, Magda, "all gussied up, with her hair in a bun, wearing this black voile dress, a rhinestone pin, and little, rimless spectacles that I associate to this day with 'looking European.'"[4] Then they picked up Diego and his bongo drums, "with his thin black mustache and his electric-blue, fitted shirt with bloused sleeves."[5] They were on their way to Ron's house that was in this "redneck sub-division, in a ranch-style house with a post-oak in the lawn."[6] They were joined by Butch and Julius who were beboppers. When they arrived, Ron was "barefoot, wearing a sleeveless Marine Corps T-shirt and camouflage fatigues."[7]

This odd assemblage began to play, led by the clarinet of Dave's father. The scene is observed in this way:

> By this time, the room was very mellow and autumnal. Ruby light angled through the windows, glowing in the drifting strata of second-hand ganja as Ron counted off the song. He and Julius started along, insinuating the Duke's sneaky, cosmopolitan shuffle. Then Magda laid down the rhythm signature. Butch and my dad came in, and played the song straight, flat out. Then they relaxed

---

3. Hickey, *Air Guitar*, 32.
4. Hickey, *Air Guitar*, 32.
5. Hickey, *Air Guitar*, 32.
6. Hickey, *Air Guitar*, 33.
7. Hickey, *Air Guitar*, 33.

the tempo, moved back to the top and let Diego croon his way through the sublime economy of Johnny Mercer's lyrics—calling up for all of us (even me) the ease and sweet sophistication of the Duke's utopian Harlem, wherein we all dwelt at the moment.[8]

Everyone shared the beat. Everyone got solo time. Everyone was responsible for a particular part. It all came together in an instant of limitless well-being. Hickey is able to see his dad "as the guy who could collect all these incongruous people around him and make sure everybody got their solos."[9] He observes "that such a genre of art lacks any institutional guarantee and must be selected by us."[10] It only flourishes in an atmosphere of generosity and agreement, and it yields acceptance and forgiveness. "Kindness, comedy, and forgiving tristesse are not the norm. They signify our little victories—and working toward democracy consists of nothing more or less than the daily accumulation of little victories whose uncommon loveliness we must, somehow, speak or show."[11] Hickey observes that such victories are not normal:

> Normal for human creatures is, and always has been a condition of inarticulate, hopeless, never-ending pain, patriarchal oppression, boredom, and violence.[12]

But artists like Norman Rockwell and Johnny Mercer resist that normal, and show us in acute ways, "Hey! People are different. Get used to it."[13] It strikes me that Hickey's scene is a performance of "all sorts and conditions of men [and women]," bound together in affliction and in hope.

When I reflected on how it is that all sorts and conditions of men and women can come together and make music together, it may not surprise you that I was led to the book of Revelation with its singing hosts. For all our misconstruals of the book, the book of Revelation is a severe, unrestrained act of imagination that traces out a world that is alternative to the stratified world of the Roman Empire that has reduced everyone to a commodity, and that refuses the wondrous freedom and generosity of genuine community. This vision in the book of Revelation is neither "other-worldly"

8. Hickey, *Air Guitar*, 35.
9. Hickey, *Air Guitar*, 35.
10. Hickey, *Air Guitar*, 38.
11. Hickey, *Air Guitar*, 38.
12. Hickey, *Air Guitar*, 39.
13. Hickey, *Air Guitar*, 40.

escapism nor is it about life after death. It is rather an act of insistent imagination that competes with and resists the imposing world of Rome. (In our context, that world is now articulated through limitless capitalist greed and unrestrained white supremacy.)

What stands out for me in this alternatively imagined world is the oft-reiterated formula of John, the writer of the book:

> You were slaughtered and by your blood you ransomed for God saints from every tribe and language and people and nation; you have made them to be a kingdom and priests serving our God, and they will reign on earth. (Rev 5:9–10)

> After this I looked, and there was a great multitude that no one could count, from every nation, from all tribes and peoples and languages, standing before the throne and before the Lamb, robed in white, with palm branches in their hands. They cried out in a loud voice. (7:9–10)

> [The beast] was allowed to make war on the saints and to conquer them. It was given authority over every tribe and people and language and nation. (13:7)

> Then I saw another angel flying in midheaven, with an eternal gospel to proclaim to those who live on the earth—to every nation and tribe and language and people. He said in a loud voice, "Fear God and give him glory, for the hour of his judgment has come; and worship him who made heaven and earth, the sea and the springs of water." (14:6–7)

> The waters that you saw, where the whore is seated, are peoples and multitudes and nations and languages. (17:15)

This may strike you, dear reader, as excessive repetition for a brief meditation. I can assure you that John did not find it excessively repetitious. He found it necessary and dramatically compelling to repeat the formula as many times as possible and to turn it in as many different directions as he could imagine for a variety of articulations. The phrase "peoples, languages, and nations" recognizes the significant variations in humanity in all its differentiations, while at the same time its elemental commonality. All have in common the dread rule of Rome. All have in common the hope for something better than the rule of Rome. All belong inescapably to the rule of the Holy One who will, soon or late, ever again, override the humanity-suffocating rule of Rome. We can thus imagine a great company of vulnerable humanity coming to terms with the cosmic combat between Rome and the God bodied in the Lamb. John—and this varied assemblage—have no doubt about the outcome of that mighty struggle in which we are engaged. And so the whole company sings in confident doxology:

> The kingdom of the world has become the kingdom of our Lord
> and of his Messiah,
> and he will reign forever and ever. (Rev 11:15)
>
> Hallelujah!
> Salvation and glory and power to our God,
> for his judgments are true and just;
> he has judged the great whore who corrupted the earth with her fornication,
> and he has avenged on her the blood of his servants. (19:1–2)

These three articulations come together for me:

- "all sorts and conditions of men and women" in the prayer;
- the assemblage of jazz music makers with Dave and his dad, just south of Fort Worth; and
- the great singing company around John anticipating the fall of Rome.

All of these are glimpses of a common humanity caught in affliction, gathered in hope, prepared to stage, in brief moments, an alternative world of wellbeing that is an act of defiance and hope. Thus the prayer is an act of hope for "a happy issue." The jazz-making is a respite from a world of work and obligation. And the news from John is a refusal to let the rulers of this world have a last say about our common destiny.

So consider:

- the church is a community that regularly prays this prayer;
- the church is regularly a potential host for jazz as the church was the original venue for good music that serves as an alternative to our unbearable "normalcy." It may host jazz as a venue for the freedom of the gospel;
- the church is the primary reader of these scriptural texts, even when they are badly misread.

- The church is a host and practitioner of this alternative world of freedom, wellbeing, and "a happy issue." It invites "all sorts and conditions of men and women" around the news and around the "meal" and may, for an instant, embody the alternative world that is intended by the holy God.

Of course the church is summoned to be at the forefront of these moments of alternative community. It is the church that is called and dispatched to be embracive of every language, people, nation and tribe. It is the church that is to be the venue for making glad music whereby we may soar past our divisive ideologies and our mutual processes of excluding the other. It is the church that is to violate all of these old divisions and separatenesses of race, class, gender, nation, and national origin. Thus:

> We are not divided, all one body we,
> one in hope and doctrine,
> one in charity.[14]

It is to be admitted that the church rarely performs this task with freedom and imagination. All too often, the church is simply an echo of an imposed ideology, whether the false absolutes of conservatism, liberalism, white supremacy, capitalist greed, or whatever. But it need not be this way! It can be a community that refuses all such distortion, and that makes sure that every participant gets a solo part at the right time.

The gathering envisioned in the book of Revelation is not "pie in the sky." It is not the-end-of-the-world speculation. Rather, it is a script for an alternative here and now. This bold imagery of the saints is a defiance of Caesar and every other ideological absolute. At its best the church's singing is not trite or innocent. It is subversive. It gives voice to a sub-version of reality that declares all dominant versions of reality are false. I reckon that Magda and her companions knew that very well, even if they could not articulate it. That is why their moments together were occasions of grace, freedom, and exuberance—an alternative world indeed!

---

14. Baring-Gould, "Onward Christian Soldiers."

Bibliography

Baring-Gould, Sabine. "Onward Christian Soldiers." 1865.
Brueggemann, Walter. "A Music-Making Counter-Community." *Church Anew*, May 2, 2023. https://churchanew.org/brueggemann/a-music-making-counter-community.
Episcopal Church. *The Book of Common Prayer*. New York: Seabury, 1977.
Hickey, Dave. *Air Guitar: Essays on Art and Democracy*. Los Angeles: Art Issues, 1997.

Conclusion

Belonging in the Valley for Dry Bones

DUSTIN D. BENAC, ERIN WEBER-JOHNSON, GLEN BELL

> [The spirit of the Lord] set me down in the middle of a valley; it was full of bones. He led me all around them; there were very many lying in the valley, and they were very dry. He said to me, "Mortal, can these bones live?" (Ezek 37–13)
>
> All were amazed and perplexed, saying to one another, "What does this mean?" But others sneered and said, "They are filled with wine." (Acts 2:13)

BELONGING IS THE AIR we breathe. The meditations in this volume describe the holy-yet-ordinary call to belonging, which is a call to life, that permeates our lives and communities. We cannot exist, individually or collectively without belonging, and we live each day in a state of dependence on others, giving and receiving the belonging we need to survive. In this time of transition in American religious life, these meditations have taken us up to the mountain top by inviting us to see a pathway for belonging that can carry us forward.

Even though belonging is the air we breathe, we do not always feel this life-giving reality in our communities and in our lives. The meditations in this volume have also borne witness, through stories and lived experience, to the fragility of our lives and our communities. We exist in a time and spaces that do not always give life, leaving the most vulnerable and fragile among us without the belonging they need. These meditations also chronicle how each of us, in seen and unseen ways, long for belonging, yet we do not always experience the life-giving reality we need. And even as individuals negotiate the shifting structures of belonging, these meditations paint a picture of the broader institutional and collective recalibration of belonging. As we are all looking for a people and a place to call home, we're simultaneously stewarding and leading institutions that are navigating shifting economic, social, and religious changes. Our lives, communities, and institutions all need belonging to survive and thrive.

Belonging Amid Dry Bones

As we reflect on our lives, we yearn for belonging, especially in times and spaces where belonging is far from us. Instead of being in spaces that call us to life, we find ourselves with Ezekiel in a valley of dry bones, cut off, isolated, and feeling in the deepest parts of our being the absence of belonging, the absence of life. This valley can prompt us to question our calling, to question our place in the world, and to question the very life-giving reality of belonging that carried us to this space. And yet, much like the work of the Spirit in Ezekiel, the pathway to belonging may pass right through the middle of this valley. As one translation expresses it, "[The Lord] led me back and forth among them." We may find ourselves lingering amid spaces that do not evoke life. While these spaces may remain places of memory and meaning, they are not marked by the life-giving reality of belonging. They take this air out of our lungs, pressing us under the weight of an unbearable existence, and leading us to wonder if our bones will simply be added to the pile alongside others. The weight will become too much to bear, the costs too great, and our presence in this space will be our final witness.

And then the LORD asks: "Mortal, can these bones live?" This is the very question we long to know when the pathway of belonging passes through the spaces where belonging is absent. Can these spaces live? Is life possible when it seems that systems and structures exist to smother it? Is there space for a life-giving call to belonging when the shifting economies only heighten competition? And is it even possible to have encounters across differences amid mounting polarization and vilification on seemingly every side? Can these bones live?

With Ezekiel, we must first heed how we are addressed: we are mortal. Our lives, our communities, and our institutions will always carry the characteristic damage of their creaturely existence. We are called to life, but we will also one day die. We are mortal, and our bones, our frailties, and our propensity to withhold the very belonging others need to survive are the same as every other mortal being.

Then an invitation comes: "Prophesy to these dry bones." In the valley of dry bones, when belonging is far from us and we are struggling to breathe, we are invited to speak: to release air from our lungs, to release to others what has given life to us, and in doing so to express our dependence on God and on one another. Our breath and our speech is active participation in God's ongoing entanglement with the world. It is a silent act of remembering who we are and the hopeful future God invites us into.

The meditations in *Pathways to Belonging* are offered in this prophetic tradition: they seek to offer life-giving words to a world when the outcome is unknown. They seek to provide a local witness that puts back together the scattered pieces of our lives and communities. Calling upon the memory of "Ancestors" in Part I, we've considered how belonging is the question of a generation and the question of all generations. Part II, "Identity" considered how identity both informs belonging and is formed through particular practices of belonging. Seeking to acknowledge the risks that are inherent to belonging, Part III, "Risks," spoke to the vulnerability that is bound in the work of belonging and the risk each of these authors took in offering their words. Part IV, "Practice," then identified particular behaviors, traditions, and contextual frameworks for fostering belonging, because belonging is carried by the embodied and collective things we do together. The pathway then turned to "Barriers and Rupture" in Part V, as we sought to tell the truth about the obstacles to belonging in our lives and in our communities. Finally, Part VI, "Creation," provided life-giving on-ramps through various channels towards newness, innovation, and shared purpose. Amid the contemporary crisis of belonging and our individual and collective longing for belonging, this, we think, is a pathway to release and reclaim the air we breathe: Ancestors. Identity. Risk. Practices. Barriers and Rupture. Creation.

Even when the pathway takes us through the spaces of desolation, to valleys of dry bones, our words can bear witness to the invitation to belonging: In God, we belong to each other, and we can build cultures of belonging with and for others.

Belonging and Structure

But there is more to the story. After the rattling of the bones following the prophet's words, a second invitation comes: "Prophesy to the breath, prophesy mortal, and say to the breath: Thus says the Lord God; Come from the four winds, O Breath, and breathe upon these slain, that they may live" (Ezek 37:9). If we follow the narrative arc of the story, it offers a vision where the breath of life can only come when a supporting structure is in place.

Just as air requires a body in order to become breath, belonging requires corresponding structures in order to give life. This, too, is the invitation of this volume. *Pathways to Belonging* is seeking to imagine, cultivate, and embody ways of being together that are distinguished by the reality of belonging. Building and inhabiting structures of this kind are certainly creative and collective acts, but they are also acts that take time and require ongoing attention and care in the particular places and institutions people serve. Accordingly, we think the pathway to belonging will always lead individuals back to the particular and local places, communities, and institutions they serve, believing that these are the concrete geographies where the structures of belonging take on flesh.

If belonging is the measure of our lives, we are always more than our outcomes, outputs, and utility. When our work is offered and our words are spoken, our efforts may or may not return with life. Nonetheless, in offering them, each of us gives voice to the alternatives we imagine. We bear witness to the future world and work as we see it.

Belonging in the Spirit

Finally, the Spirit is a companion and guide on the pathways to belonging. If we turn to Acts 2, we see a similar story where belonging is breaking forth. We likely know the story well: a great wind comes at Pentecost, tongues of fire descend on those who were gathered, the Holy Spirit fills each of them such that they begin speaking in tongues, and individuals in the crowd then hear them speaking in their native language. This scene is, as Willie James Jennings notes, "the beginning of a community broken upon by the sheer act of God, and we are yet to comprehend the extent to which God acts and is acting to break us open."[1]

---

1. Jennings, *Acts*, 27–28.

Just as we cannot walk these pathways of belonging without others, we cannot offer words and work that creates space for belonging without the Spirit. We exist in a dance of dependence, receiving the gift of belonging from God and offering the breath of belonging to others. The meditations offered here and the collaboration that guide this volume emerge from a posture of creative dependence, seeking to understand and explore the depths of belonging we share. They bear witness to how much better we are together, and the ways we can continue to image and cultivate belonging amid the places and people we serve.

Before we conclude with an invitation, there is one final thread we need to leave unresolved: creative acts to deepen the ties of belonging may not be embraced or celebrated by others. As the narrative notes: "All were amazed and perplexed, saying to one another, 'What does this mean?' But others sneered and said, 'They are filled with new wine'" (Acts 2:13). While the Ezekiel story provides a climatic resolution, the bones are remade and bodies take on flesh, the outcome is muted here. People respond in a variety of ways: amazement, puzzled, and sneering. A new way of being together is emerging, but the crowds do not respond in a way that sees or gives space for life.

We think this range of response is also part of the pathway to belonging. As we offer our holy-yet-ordinary life-giving work into the world, some will respond with wonder, others will be puzzled, and some will sneer. Even when we extend the gift of belonging to others, our words and work are not always met with the same invitation to life. Even though we long to create space where others can receive the gift of belonging they long for, we cannot give them eyes to see and receive our work or our presence as the gift that it is. And even when our work along the pathway to belonging is met with resistance, the Spirit will still carry our collective hope forward.

An Invitation

Wherever you find yourself on a pathway to belonging, we want to conclude with a simple invitation. First, you are not alone. Amid the isolation, precarity, polarization, and despair that marks so many communities, we often find ourselves wandering in lonely and desolate spaces. Even though faith leaders seek to kindle hope, it can be difficult to hold the fire of hope ourselves. We offer these simple collected words to you in hopes that you will find traveling companions, words to keep you company, and guides to support your work as you discern the next step.

Second, in offering this collective of meditations, we invite you to write your own meditation on belonging that bears witness to the wisdom that you and your community carry. We've purposefully provided a structure to guide your reflects and individual's work building and imagining the belonging that gives life. Guided by the story of Scripture and the work or prophets and teachings that have come before us, we think the craft of weighing and writing words is a practice that gives life. And if you take the risk of writing in some form, we hope you will take the chance of sharing your written words with someone near to you at the right time.

Finally, we hope you will join us in our ongoing work creating and sustaining cultures of belonging in the communities we serve. We have done this work because we think it is a time to build communities and structures that will nourish and carry our peoples for a generation. Amid a time of great uncertainty and reordering, the belonging we cherish often feels like it is slipping through our fingers, or it is fleeting, just out of reach. The words in this volume, however, tell a different story. Even while belonging can at times be fragile and even frail, it is a reality we can seek, cultivate, and pursue. And through the ongoing work of God, community, and Spirit, belonging remains a gift that we can receive and offer to others.

Guided by this reality, we invite you to walk these pathways of belonging with us, and with others.

Bibliography

Jennings, Willie James. *Acts: A Theological Commentary on the Bible.* Louisville, KY: Westminster John Knox, 2017.

www.ingramcontent.com/pod-product-compliance
Lightning Source LLC
Chambersburg PA
CBHW031429150426
43191CB00006B/452